THERAPEUTIC TOUCH

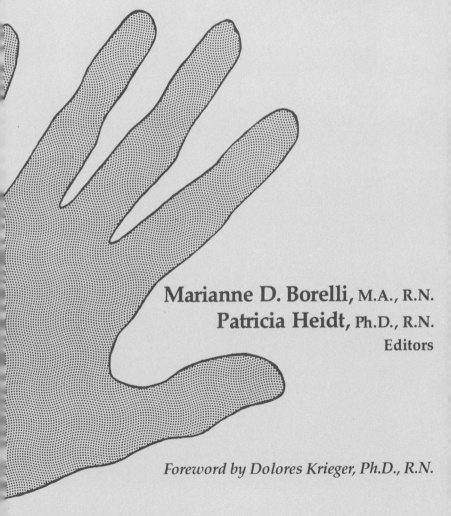

Marianne D. Borelli, M.A., R.N.
Patricia Heidt, Ph.D., R.N.
Editors

Foreword by Dolores Krieger, Ph.D., R.N.

THERAPEUTIC TOUCH

A Book of Readings

Marianne D. Borelli, M.A., R.N.
Patricia Heidt, Ph.D., R.N.
Editors

SPRINGER PUBLISHING COMPANY
New York

Springer Publishing Company, Inc.
200 Park Avenue South
New York, New York 10003

81 82 83 84 85 / 10 9 8 7 6 5 4 3 2 1

Library of Congress Cataloging in Publication Data

Main entry under title:

Therapeutic touch.

    Includes bibliographies and index.
    1.   Mental healing—Addresses, essays, lectures.
I.   Borelli, Marianne D.   II.   Heidt, Patricia.
RZ400.T38   615.8′52   80-14109
ISBN 0-8261-3110-7
ISBN 0-8261-3111-5 (pbk.)

Printed in the United States of America

Contents

Foreword

Dolores Krieger, Ph.D., R.N.

Therapeutic Touch: A Book of Readings stresses the individual, personal nature of intervention through the practice of Therapeutic Touch. I am delighted to have this opportunity to voice my general concurrence with this emphasis.

It has become evident to me during ten years of postdoctoral research, clinical practice, and teaching of Therapeutic Touch that there are three factors that ensure the safe and successful practice of Therapeutic Touch: (1) intention, (2) motivation, and (3) personal recognition and acceptance by the practitioner of the reason he/she wants to play the role of healer.

Intention connotes a clear formulation of goal; it suggests that the Therapeutic Touch practitioner should have a lucid concept of how to help/heal, as well as the mere desire to do so. The practitioner's motivation, of course, provides the psychodynamic thrust, the direction that this healing/helping act will take and, therefore, it colors the emotional tone of the dyadic relationship between healer and healee. Finally, it is important for the practitioner to understand his/her own drives in wanting to play the role of healer. It does not matter what these drives are; what is important is that the practitioner willingly recognize the personal foundations for his/her involvement in this highly personalized interaction.

All of these factors imply that the Therapeutic Touch practitioner accepts responsibility for his/her own method of helping/healing. Healing is a natural potential in all persons that can be actualized under the appropriate circumstances.

It is my good fortune to know most of the authors of this book of readings. Their personal accounts reveal their individual growth through the practice of Therapeutic Touch, one of the most humane of all human interactions. Perceptive readers will learn much from these accounts and will be able to use them as models for their own development of Therapeutic Touch practices.

March 1, 1980

Preface

Despite the extensive capabilities of Western health care systems, they are often found lacking by the consumer. One of the most frequent criticisms of such systems is that human caring has been set aside and the cause of scientific advancement has taken precedence. Interactions between patient and practitioner are often brief, impersonal, and mechanistic. The human exchange has in many cases been superseded by the emphasis on efficient, scientific treatment of deviations from health. The image of the family doctor or of the bedside nurse who knew and cared for patients individually is a cherished memory for many people.

Traditional health care systems also fail to take into account the complex interactions between mind, body, and environment. Findings concerning the nature of mind–body–environment interaction within the areas of biofeedback, meditation, biological rhythmicity, and imagery in the treatment of disease indicate the fallacy of being concerned with only the manifest symptoms of deviations from health. The supposition that one's state of mind has a profound effect on the individual's state of wellness or illness is becoming widely accepted, as is evidenced by the increased body of research in psychosomatic health care (Lipowski, 1977).

This approach to understanding man as a complex mind–body–environment interaction is termed *holistic*. The fragmented treatment of isolated symptoms without consideration of this complex interaction is disclaimed by holism. In a holistic approach to treatment such factors as diet, stress level, life satisfaction, life change, and environmental pollution are taken into account. In addition, the holistic view acknowledges that man has more responsibility and control over his state of wellness or illness than has been previously acknowledged. The maintenance and restoration of health is seen as not merely the responsibility of the practitioner but also that of the patient.

It is within this holistic framework that Therapeutic Touch can be viewed. According to Krieger (1973, p. 1), "Therapeutic Touch is a derivative of laying-on of hands in that it uses the hands to direct excess body energies from a person playing the role of the healer to a person who is ill for the purpose of helping or healing that individual." Therapeutic Touch differs from the laying-on of hands in that it is not performed within a religious context and is not dependent upon the faith of the healer or the one being healed (hereinafter called the "healee"). Therapeutic Touch is performed by the healer in a state of centeredness and with intentionality for the enhancement of the well-being of the healee.

Therapeutic Touch is based upon the assumption that the body is an energy field which is continually affecting and being influenced by fields outside itself. With such a view of man and his relationship to his environment, energy transfer between individuals becomes plausible. This assumption is not new. It has been recognized for some time that the human body is an energy field and that activity in the neuromuscular system occurs by means of electrical conductance. The body as an energy field has been the focus of intensive study by Burr (1972), who found field changes in patients as their physical and emotional conditions changed. These findings suggest that body fields are more pervasive and complex than merely the electrical impulses of the neuromuscular system.

One's frame of reference for performing Therapeutic Touch must then include the notion of man as an energy field, engaged in a continual interaction with other fields in the environment. It is by developing one's sensitivities to the body field that one learns to get a sense of its condition and to transfer energy to the healee. This issue of energy exchange between healer and healee will be taken up in later chapters of this book.

Interactions between persons during Therapeutic Touch are personal and focused. Therapeutic Touch is a profoundly human exchange between a person in the role of the healer and another as healee. The intent to help another is the foundation for its practice. As an adjunct to conventional medical care, the act of Therapeutic Touch can provide additional means for helping the person who is ill. The ability to transfer energy in Therapeutic Touch is believed by Krieger (1979) to be a human potential which is activated by the motivation to help another. One of the first things to be developed is the ability to center oneself, that is, to find within the self a place of stability and self-relatedness. This state of centeredness must be maintained throughout the healing interactions. This enables the healer to focus on the healee with less distraction, to become aware of changes in sensory cues in the hands which indicate the state of the field, and to direct and moderate the outflow of energy to the person in need.

Learning to use Therapeutic Touch is not the same as mastering a technique. It is a process which involves intensive self-searching as to the reasons one wants to help another. It is a growth process, transcending ego needs, during which one learns about the self by learning to find a place of stability or center within oneself. It is also a gradual development of greater sensitivity to the energy field of another through which one learns to perceive the physical and emotional needs of the person. And, through practice, it is the development of confidence in one's judgments about the condition of the field and about the manner of energy transfer.

Therapeutic Touch is built on the pioneering efforts of Dora Kunz, whose observations led to the original conceptualization of Therapeutic Touch, and of Dolores Krieger, whose research has been the basis for the development of the theoretical model of Therapeutic Touch. For the past ten years, Dr. Krieger, who is a professor of nursing at New York University, has been conducting post-doctoral research on Therapeutic Touch. She has also instituted the master's level course on Therapeutic Touch at New York University, "Frontiers in Nursing: The Actualization of Potential for Therapeutic Human Field Interaction." She has taught Therapeutic Touch to almost 350 professional nurses in this course as well as given numerous seminars and workshops to over 4,000 health care professionals in the United States and Canada. For a more detailed, first person account of the historical development and the process involved in this healing intervention, the reader is referred to Dr. Krieger's book, *The Therapeutic Touch: How to Use Your Hands to Help or to Heal.*

The articles in this book of readings on Therapeutic Touch are an outgrowth of the theoretical framework which Krieger and Kunz have developed. This collection presents the existing research upon which Therapeutic Touch rests, and in addition, explores current clinical applications of Therapeutic Touch in a variety of settings. It is the purpose of the authors not to make a definitive statement regarding Therapeutic Touch, but to provide an open forum for sharing research and experiences in this area. The area of Therapeutic Touch is in a state of early development and it is intended that this book will enhance the developmental process.

It will become obvious to the reader that each author writes from his/ her own personal synthesis of the existing knowledge of Therapeutic Touch. Each author's interpretation of healing and thus of Therapeutic Touch differs slightly. This is in concert with the aim of this book, which is to provide a network of communication for both patients and clinicians who are interested in sharing their knowledge about and experiences with this healing modality.

The book will be divided into three sections: (1) theoretical foundations of Therapeutic Touch, (2) current research and clinical applications of Therapeutic Touch, and (3) patient's responses to Therapeutic Touch.

Marianne D. Borelli

References

Burr, H. *Blueprint for immortality: the electric patterns of life.* London: Neville-Spearman, 1972.

Krieger, D. The relationship of touch, with intent to help and heal, to subject's in-vivo hemoglobin values: a study in personalized interaction. In *Proceedings of the ninth ANA nursing research conference.* Kansas City: American Nurses' Associaion, 1973, p.1.

Krieger, D. *The Therapeutic Touch: how to use your hands to help or to heal.* Englewood Cliffs, N.J.: Prentice-Hall, 1979.

Lipowski, Z. Psychosomatic medicine in the seventies: An overview. *American Journal of Psychiatry*, 1977, *134*, 233–243.

Contributors

Rene Beck is affiliated with the Psychology Department of San Francisco State University and is a biofeedback trainer at the Stress Reduction Center of Marin in California.

Marianne D. Borelli, M.A., R.N., is a doctoral candidate, Division of Nursing, New York University. She has worked in the areas of medical/surgical and psychiatric nursing and has taught psychiatric nursing at the baccalaureate level.

Philip Caleb, a retired Major, USAF, is a graduate student in counseling at Adelphi University in New York.

Diana Finnerin, M.A., R.N., is assistant professor at the County College of Morris, Division of Nursing, Randolph, New Jersey.

Honore Fontes, M.A., R.N., is an instructor as well as a doctoral candidate in the Division of Nursing, New York University.

Mary Jean Gallagher is a practicing attorney who lives in Upper Montclair, New Jersey. She has begun training at a psychoanalytic institute in New York City.

Patricia Heidt, Ph.D., R.N., is a psychotherapist in private practice in both New York City and New Paltz, New York. She lectures and conducts workshops on Therapeutic Touch and other aspects of holistic health care.

Mary E. Mueller Jackson, M.A., R.N., is currently employed at Rush Presbyterian, St. Luke's Medical Center, and Johnston R. Bowman Health Center for the Elderly in Chicago. She specializes in chronic and terminal care of the elderly.

Anne Marie H. Jonasen, R.N., is a nurse educator and practitioner of Therapeutic Touch and is an operating room specialist in Berkeley, California.

Christina Lukasiewicz, R.N., is a doctoral candidate in nursing education, Columbia University, New York.

Janet Macrae, M.A., R.N., is a practitioner and teacher of Therapeutic Touch and meditation, as well as a doctoral candidate in nursing at New York University.

Marsha Jane Nagelberg-Gerhard, M.A., R.N., is a nurse/healer and is active in her private holistic health practice. She teaches at Rutgers University, College of Nursing, and is completing her Ph.D. at New York University.

Erik Peper, Ph.D., is director of the Biofeedback and Family Therapy Institute, Berkeley, California. He is also coauthor of *Mind/Body: Essential Readings in Biofeedback* and *From the Inside Out: Self-Teaching Laboratory Manual for Biofeedback.* He is affiliated with the Center for Interdisciplinary Science, San Francisco State University.

Martin Proudfoot, M.D., is a physician in family practice in Edmonds, Washington.

Janet Quinn, M.A., R.N., is an instructor of nursing at Hunter College— Bellvue School of Nursing and a doctoral candidate at New York University.

Joey Upland, B.S., R.N., is a nurse/healer working in San Quentin Prison and is codirector of the Institute for Stress and Pain Management, San Francisco.

Renée Weber, Ph.D., is professor of philosophy at Rutgers University where she teaches oriental philosophy. She has published on the esoteric and holistic traditions in philosophy, and on the holographic theory of reality.

Iris Wolfson, R.N., is a childbirth educator for the Association for Childbirth at Home and is a home birth attendant.

PART I

Theoretical Foundations

When studying any phenomenon it is essential to look first at the events and trends which preceded it and influenced its emergence. The preface has presented the trends in health care that have allowed for the rediscovery of a very ancient healing modality now more specifically defined as Therapeutic Touch. In this section the reader is presented with a comprehensive review of the existing research, both scientific and philosophical, which has been done on healing by the laying-on of hands and Therapeutic Touch.

In Western culture, scrutiny by the scientific method has become the rite of passage by which phenomena are given scientific credibility. Heidt's review of the existing research in this section gives the reader a developmental approach to the scientific study of laying-on of hands and Therapeutic Touch. This is, however, not the only vantage point for the study of Therapeutic Touch. Another perspective is given by Borelli's discussion of meditation as the necessary mental state of the healer during Therapeutic Touch. Between those two is Weber's synthesis of the philosophical systems compatible with healing, which represents a pioneering attempt to explore and develop a paradigm for healing.

Chapter 1

Scientific Research
and Therapeutic Touch

Patricia Heidt

Although the history of laying-on of hands goes back to early historical times, the scientific investigation of healing is very recent. The
purpose of this chapter is to present that body of research upon
which Therapeutic Touch was developed.

Early Scientific
Investigation on Healing

Bernard Grad (1965) wrote how paradoxical it was that although research methodology existed to find the answers as to why "unorthodox methods of healing" produced their effects, these techniques
were not utilized. Since the "power of suggestion" was usually offered as the answer, investigators had no interest in examining such
phenomena. Grad (1961), who was a biochemist at McGill University, collaborated with R. V. Cadoret and G. I. Paul of the University
of Manitoba in an experiment to demonstrate that there was more
than "suggestion" involved in the laying-on of hands.

Three hundred mice of the same size and weight were
"wounded" by cutting out an oval of skin 0.4 by 0.8 inches along
the spine of the animal. They were randomly assigned to one of
three treatment groups. The first group received treatment that
consisted of Oskar Estabany, a world-renowned healer, holding the
caged mice between his hands for a 15-minute period of time two
times daily, five hours apart. A second group of mice received a

3

similar treatment; however, medical students who did not claim to be "healers" administered this treatment. As a control, a third group of mice remained undisturbed on a table during the treatment period.

Each treatment group of mice was assigned to separate rooms on a random basis. The individuals who were randomly assigned to their care were unaware of which group of mice was assigned to the three treatment groups. Treatment was administered in three adjacent rooms, similar in size, temperature, and humidity. Before the treatment period, cages were put into paper bags, picked up by "transfer men" and brought to the treatment room. After treatment, the cages were returned to their paper bags, and again returned to their home rooms by "transfer men."

During the treatment period, the caged mice were placed inside opaque paper bags. In half of the mice in each group, the bag was left open and the hands of Estabany or the other "healers" were inserted inside the bag and the treatment cages held directly between the hands without the healers looking at the mice. In the other half of the mice, the paper bags were stapled shut, and the healer's hands were placed on top of the paper bag, preventing direct contact with the treatment cage.

To assess the effects of treatment, a two-way analysis of variance was used. On the 15th and 16th day after wounding, the mean surface area of the wounds in the group of mice treated by Estabany were significantly smaller than those of the other two groups in the "open bag" series.

It was found that mice in the closed bags were particularly agitated, apparently due to lack of air. Grad's earlier pilot investigations had found that nervous animals were less responsive to the laying-on of hands and for this reason the practice of "gentling" the animals prior to wounding was undertaken. The lesser response of these animals was therefore not a surprising result. Grad notes that the gentling or stroking of the animals was done before the experiment, and to the mice in all three treatment groups. None of the gentling was done by Mr. Estabany. The possibility that heat could account for the observed effects was ruled out because the second group of mice was also exposed to the heat of the medical students' hands.

A second series of experiments by Grad (1964, 1967) involved Mr. Estabany treating barley seeds that had been soaked in saline to simulate a "sick condition." These double-blind studies gave evidence that the group of plants watered by a one percent sodium chloride solution which had been placed in a stoppered beaker and held by Estabany for 15 minutes daily differed significantly from the other two treatment groups, in number of seedlings, mean height, and mean yield of plant material.

Grad (1965) experimented with other healers than Estabany and found that there were significant results, "some of them in the positive direction and others in the opposite direction," demonstrating that healing abilities were not confined to "single or very few individuals" (p. 124). Grad stated that at this time, although his experiments demonstrated that laying-on of hands accelerated wound healing in mice and stimulated the growth of barley seeds, they did not answer the "what" or "how" of the process.

It was in 1967 that Smith, another biochemist, reasoned that if enzyme failure is the ultimate physical cause of disease, healing should take place at the same level, i.e., it should be detected in enzyme activity. In her laboratory at Rosary Hill College, Buffalo, she set up a double-blind study using the enzyme trypsin (1972). Solutions of trypsin were divided into four flasks: one was retained untreated as the control. A second was held by Estabany (the same healer as above) in the manner that he did laying-on of hands with patients (in this situation, putting his hands around the stoppered flask for 75 minutes). A third flask of trypsin was exposed to ultraviolet light to "damage" the protein for sufficient time to reduce the activity 68–80 percent, and then it was held by Estabany. A fourth solution was exposed to a high magnetic field (8,000–13,000 gauss).

The results of her experiment indicated that the exposure of the trypsin solution to the laying-on of hands as performed by Estabany was "qualitatively and quantitatively similar to that of a magnetic field" (Smith, 1972, p. 18). Later that same year, the research was repeated using the same experimental design but involving healers other than Estabany. Three people claimed to have healing power and three did not. None of these subjects had a positive effect on the enzymes.

In 1971 the study was replicated with three other "paranormal healers." Results varied quantitatively each day with each of the healers, such variations being correlated with the physical and/or environmental state of the psychics. Qualitative effects, i.e., the increase in enzyme activity, did consistently increase. Other enzyme systems were introduced into the research: NAD (nicotin-amide-adenine-dinucleotide) and amylose-amylase. When the healers treated the first enzyme, NAD, there was a decrease in activity. None of the healers effected a change in activity rate of the amylose-amylase. The results of such studies indicated that not all enzymes were affected by the healers' abilities in the same way and that some enzymes were not affected at all (Smith, 1972).

Research in Therapeutic Touch

Dolores Krieger, a Professor of Nursing at New York University, was the first to study the laying-on of hands in human subjects. She had observed Estabany's healing abilities and the effects that he had with patients during several healing seminars. She also was a student of Dora Kunz, a woman who had participated in healing experimentation because of her remarkable abilities to perceive the human energy field (Karagulla, 1967).

Krieger (1973) hypothesized that hemoglobin would be a sensitive indicator of energy change as well as of oxygen uptake and would be an appropriate test object in human subjects who were treated by the laying-on of hands. Krieger noted that the porphyrin structure of the hemoglobin molecule (which is responsible for oxygen uptake in the tissues) resembles the chlorine structure of chlorophyll in that both are derivative of the same biosynthetic pathways, and that the nature and arrangement of their side chains are similar. Whereas the chlorophyll molecule is patterned around an atom of magnesium, the porphyrin in hemoglobin is patterned around an atom of iron. The prior findings of Grad (1964) had indicated that there was an increased chlorophyll content in the barley sprouts treated by water held by Estabany. Research by Smith (1972) had also indicated that enzyme systems responded to laying-on of hands. The biosynthesis of hemoglobin is dependent on numerous enzymatic transactions, among them ALA synthetase,

ALA dehydratase, and ferriochelatase, and thus hemoglobin was chosen as the dependent variable for her experiments.

Following initial pilot studies, Krieger utilized 46 subjects in the experimental group and 29 subjects in the control group. All subjects were controlled for the following variables: pretest hemoglobin values, circadian cycles, smoking of tobacco, recent trauma, history of recent change in vital signs; all of these can significantly change hemoglobin levels. Pretest samples of blood were drawn on all subjects. Mr. Estabany again served as the healer in this experiment. Following the laying-on of hands by Estabany, posttest samples of blood were drawn from both the experimental group and the subjects in the control group. Results verified the hypothesis that posttest mean hemoglobin values in the experimental group would be greater than the pretest means at the 0.01 level of confidence (Krieger, 1973). There was no significant change in the posttest means of the control group.

Krieger supported her experimentation with a theoretical framework drawn from her study of Eastern religions. She posited that the healthy individual has an overabundance of *prana*, i.e., life force, whereas the ill person has a deficit. She noted that the Sanskrit word *prana* actually pertains to the organizing factors which underlie the life processes responsible for regeneration and healing. This life force can be transferred from one individual to another (Krieger, 1973, 1974). She conceptualized the relationship between healer and healee as follows:

> ...The healthy individual is an open system of streaming-energy subsets in constant flux....The ill person can be conceptualized as one in whom this system has closed-in, so to speak, upon himself. The role of the healer then would be concerned with helping the ill person to reestablish this vital flowing, open system to restore, as it were, unimpeded communication with his environment (Krieger, 1974, p. 125).

Krieger believed that all persons have this ability to heal and that this natural potential can be activated whenever the person in the role of healer is motivated by an interest to help the person in need. Another condition is that the healer be willing to confront honestly the reason why he/she chose to play the role of healer. At this time, Krieger called this healing intervention Therapeutic Touch, instead of laying-on of hands because there was this essential difference: Therapeutic Touch was not performed within a religious context, nor was it dependent upon the faith of the healer or the healee (1974).

In a second experiment, Krieger (1974) used a design and methodology that were similar to those in her initial study. However, this time professional registered nurses served as the "healers." Patients receiving Therapeutic Touch were in the experimental group; patients receiving routine nursing care without intervention by Therapeutic Touch were in the control group. In addition to the controls utilized in the initial research, Krieger controlled for meditational practices and breathing exercises by the subjects. She also adhered to the following delimitations: (1) The informed consent of all participating patients was obtained according to the Patient's Bill of Rights developed by the American Hospital Association. (2) The cooperation of the patient's Department of Nursing and the patient's physician were assured. (3) A request for approval and a proposal for research design was submitted to the Board of Research in each facility where one existed. (4) Blood samples in the study were analyzed only by the Coulter machine. (5) The technicians analyzing the blood samples were not informed that research was in progress.

In both the experimental and control groups, there were 32 patients and 16 nurses, each nurse working with two patients. Pretest blood samples were drawn for both hemoglobin values and hematocrit ratios on all patients. Therapeutic Touch was then administered to the experimental group on two consecutive days by nurses taught to do this intervention by Krieger and/or Kunz. Posttest samples were drawn a minimum of four hours after the last treatment by Therapeutic Touch. The data supported the hypothesis that the mean hemoglobin values of patients treated by Therapeutic Touch changed significantly following such treatment at the 0.001 level of confidence.

The Process of Therapeutic Touch

There are distinct phases in the act of Therapeutic Touch, which although presented here in serial fashion, do not always take place in this manner.

In the first phase of Therapeutic Touch, the person in the role of healer makes the intention to therapeutically assist the person in need. Then he/she "centers" the self physically and psychologically (Krieger, 1979). In this act of self-relatedness, the healer becomes aware of self as an open system of energies. Centering can be conceptualized as becoming aware of the space within oneself—that inner place where one is quiet, focused, and attentive. Therapeutic Touch has been called a "healing meditation" because during the process, the healer tries to remain focused upon the healing touch and allows all other thoughts to leave the mind (Krieger, Peper, and Ancoli, 1979).

In the next phase, the healer moves the hands over the body of the person in need from head to feet, attuning to the condition of the other by becoming aware of changes in sensory cues in the hands. This assessment allows the healer to gain information about the personal field of the ill person so that intervention can be based on as much knowledge about the ill person as possible. By the term *personal field*, Krieger (1979) refers to the fact that the human body's functions occur via electrical conductance, and there is within and surrounding the body a "field" to carry the charge.

The healer then redirects areas of accumulated tension in the ill person's field by moving the hands over the body in a sweeping gesture. This has been described as "unruffling the field" because this process facilitates the movements of the "bound" or "congested" energy in the ill person's body. Krieger (1979, p. 55) writes that although we know little at this stage about the dynamics of human field interaction, her experience of the process of "unruffling the field" indicates it to be of value in assisting the healee's field to mobilize its own resources so that self-healing may take place.

Using the hands as a focal point, the healer then directs energy to the person in need. This is based on the understanding that both healer and healee are vibrating fields of energy, sending and receiving this energy from the environment surrounding them. Because each healee's field is different, it is necessary that the healer learn to modulate this energy, i.e., temper the energy outflow to the other during this phase of the healing interaction (Krieger, 1979).

When the healer is no longer able to detect any changes in the sensory cues of his/her hands, it is time to stop. The healer, for the time being, perceives a balance in the fields of both self and healee.

The Relaxation Response
of Therapeutic Touch

Four patients from an outpatient pain-control center of a large hospital participated in laboratory experimentation on Therapeutic Touch. While receiving this intervention on two consecutive days, the recording of electroencephalographic, electromyographic, galvanic skin response, temperature, and heart rate indices revealed that all were in a relaxed state throughout the process. All patients reported they felt relaxed and enjoyed the experience, and they were willing to volunteer again (Krieger, Peper, and Ancoli, 1979).

Krieger (1979) notes that in her experience of the practice of Therapeutic Touch, there is a characteristic pattern of response which occurs in approximately 90 percent of the patients. These signs are: (1) the healee's voice level goes down several decibels, (2) the healee's respirations slow down and deepen, (3) an audible sigh of relaxation occurs, i.e., a deep breath or a sigh, or a statement such as "I feel relaxed", and (4) an observable peripheral flush may be noted on the face or on the whole body, which is due to dilatation of the peripheral vascular system during the healer-healee interaction.

Other Healer–Healee Responses

Therapeutic Touch does not claim to be a miracle cure. Because it is based on the natural laws of human field interaction, it elicits in the healee a natural healing response. It has been found to accelerate the healing processes within the individual whenever there is an imbalance of energy (Krieger, 1979). Therapeutic Touch decreases and often eliminates pain. Illnesses with a psychosomatic origin respond well to Therapeutic Touch. Krieger (1979, p. 90) notes that in her experience, Therapeutic Touch significantly affects symptoms arising from autonomic nervous system disorders, such as nausea, dyspnea, tachycardia, and pallor.

In the personal statements made by a sample of 250 healers who practiced Therapeutic Touch in the United States and in Canada, it is obvious that the experience of Therapeutic Touch has benefits for the practitioner as well as the recipient (Krieger, 1979). These anecdotes indicate that there were significant changes in the healers' (1) sense of their internal and external environment, (2) sense of energy flow, (3) emotion, (4) cognition, (5) memory, (6) sense of time, and (7) sense of personal identity.

Author's Comment:
Searching for a New Paradigm

Kuhn (1970) states that a sign of maturity in the development of any given science is the acquisition of a "paradigm." This may include the laws, theories, methodology, and instrumentation upon which scientific research is based. In the history of science, there have been crisis points in which newly discovered evidence about the nature of reality caused a blurring of the original paradigm. A period of tension then existed during which time a search for another paradigm ensued to explain this "new evidence" about man and his world. Kuhn terms the transition to new paradigms a "scientific revolution" and argues that it is the nature of science (or the universe itself) to move consistently toward new discovery and emerging world views (p. 90).

The work of Grad, Smith, and Krieger, as well as the research of some other scientists which is beyond the scope of this present text, falls into that scientific era which Kuhn calls *preparadigm* (1970, p. 77). Today there seems to be a feeling among many men and women in a variety of professional disciplines that older scientific models have failed to provide adequate solutions to the urgent problems they are facing in their personal and professional lives. As in crisis periods of the past, traditional paradigms cannot account for an increasing number of observations about man–environment relationships. Ancient and Oriental systems of consciousness, transcultural healing practices, traditions of spirituality and mysticism, as well as accumulating data from clinical and laboratory research all offer important clues for a new understanding of the nature of reality.

It is within this framework that the scientific research of Grad, Smith, Krieger, and others makes such an important contribution.

Their work is a challenge to traditional conceptual models about the nature of healing and man–environment relationships. As such, they stand as "evolutionary" as well as revolutionary landmarks toward discovering the new paradigm of reality.

Bibliography

Grad, B. Influence of unorthodox methods of treatment on wound healing in mice. *International Journal of Parapsychology*, 1961, *3*, 5–24.

Grad, B. A telekinetic effect on plant growth. II. Experiments involving treatment of saline in stoppered bottles. *International Journal of Parapsychology*, 1964, *6*, 473–485.

Grad, B. Some biological effects of the laying-on of hands. *Journal of the American Society for Psychical Research*, 1965, *59*, 95–127.

Grad, B. Laying-on of hands: implications for psychotherapy, gentling and placebo effect. *Journal of the American Society for Psychical Research*, 1967, *61*, 286–305.

Karagulla, S. *Breakthrough to creativity*. Santa Monica, Calif.: De Vorss and Company, 1967.

Krieger, D. The relationship of touch, with intent to help or to heal, to subjects' in-vivo hemoglobin values: a study in personalized interaction. In *Proceedings of the ninth ANA nursing research conference*. Kansas City: American Nurses' Association, 1973.

Krieger, D. Healing by the laying-on of hands as a facilitator of bioenergetic change: the response of in-vivo human hemoglobin. *Psychoenergetics*, 1974, *1*, 121–219.

Krieger, D. Therapeutic Touch: the imprimatur of nursing. *American Journal of Nursing*, 1975, *75*, 784–787.

Krieger, D. *The Therapeutic Touch: how to use your hands to help or to heal*. Englewood Cliffs, N.J.: Prentice-Hall, 1979.

Krieger, D., Peper, E., and Ancoli, S. Therapeutic Touch: searching for evidence of physiological change. *American Journal of Nursing*, 1979, *79*, 660–662.

Kuhn, T. *The structure of scientific revolutions*. Chicago: University of Chicago Press, 1970.

Smith, J. Paranormal effects of enzyme activity. *Human Dimensions*, 1972, *1*, 12–15.

Chapter 2

Philosophical Foundations and Frameworks for Healing

Renée Weber

*The whole universe is one mathematical and
symphonic expression, made up of finite
representations of the infinite.*
                                    —F. L. Kunz

This chapter should confess at the outset that we do not as yet
have a clear theory accounting for healing. An ideal and rigorous
explanation in terms of necessary and sufficient conditions—re-
sembling a scientific law—seems at present beyond our reach. We
must be content, therefore, with some philosophical frameworks
compatible with the phenomenon of healing. Interestingly, these
frameworks, though drawn from diverse cultures and epochs separated in time, cohere and thus possess certain common denominators. These denominators consist of a basic shared foundation,
however varied may be the structures built thereon. A foundation,
by dictionary definition, is "that on which anything is founded and
by which it is supported or sustained," or alternatively as "that part
of a building below the surface of the ground, or the portion that
constitutes its base." By contrast, a framework is "a skeleton structure for supporting or enclosing something." We may thus conclude that the several skeletal structures "enclosing" the data that
bear on various forms of healing rest, in spite of diversity, on a single

This article first appeared in *Revision: A Journal of Knowledge and Consciousness*, 2, 2, Summer-Fall, 1979.

shared foundation that makes the healing phenomenon possible in the first place. Given the specific and singular nature of that foundation, with its unique claims about man and the universe, it follows that only certain philosophical frameworks can be invoked to deal with healing, while others are incompatible with the foundation on which the healing factor rests. By "healing" I refer to a process in which a person become whole physically, emotionally, mentally, and at deeper levels, resulting ideally in an integration with the underlying inward power of the universe.

Consequently, the ensuing discussion will try to establish that the Healing Hypothesis is bound up with a major and majestic aim, transcending the mere utilitarian absence of bodily disease. Hopefully, this exploration will contribute toward an eventual Theory of Healing, despite the fact that our present attempts are necessarily rudimentary and provisional.

The theoretical and philosophical frameworks compatible with the Healing Hypothesis can sound the direction in which our further search and research must move, and some of the rich details embedded in these frameworks may turn out to be useful in this endeavor. The major task, however, still lies ahead. It consists of discovering and clearly formulating the foundation for the dynamics of healing as such: a single principle of potent explanatory and predictive scope. This task awaits a creative breakthrough in which a new paradigm of space, time, matter, energy, life, and consciousness will be forged within a unified field of knower and known.

The Healing Hypothesis

Throughout this chapter I shall use the term the *Healing Hypothesis* to refer to a total context or syndrome of factors that seem interwoven with healing. Among these are the following claims: the existence of energy and consciousness in various states, qualitatively differentiated, with supremacy over gross physical matter; the irrelevance of the Cartesian grid and hence of physical contiguity to healing, involving us instead in novel concepts of space, time, and energy; the relativity of time in various dimensions of space and its absence from the n-dimensional space of pure spiritual energy where the healing power originates; the increasing physicality and density of this energy as it enters the space–time sphere of organisms, a process in which the healer acts as a conduit. The claim of the Healing Hypothesis further involves the power of intentionality of unbounded living systems such as ourselves, ceaselessly interpenetrating one another, rather than being restricted to the discernible boundaries of our bodies and personalities; and the resultant interchange of qualitatively charged energies among all organisms in the universe, resulting in either creative or destructive consequences for the cosmic ecology, spreading order or disorder depending on the wholeness or fragmentation of those energies. Finally, it may be stated that this universal healing energy is not neutral nor value free, but is an energy of order, intelligence, and compassion (Bohm, 1978; Kunz, 1977, 1978, 1979; Weber, 1978a).

Incompatible Frameworks

A useful preliminary consideration is to examine some frameworks that cannot be invoked to explain healing. Some of these are materialism, positivism, reductionism, behaviorism, and other crude versions of physicalism. Their fundamental incompatibility with the Healing Hypothesis is that their very foundation contradicts a healing thesis as such. The central assumption shared by those movements is a selective empiricism based on 18th- and 19th-century materialistic physics. Ironically, that version of physics has now been repudiated by advances in 20th-century physics, and thus seems no longer warranted even by current developments within science (Bohm, 1978; Capra, 1975; Weber, 1975, 1978b).

In spite of this, 18th- and 19th-century views about the nature of matter and energy persist, especially in the life sciences, and these reductionistic, mechanistic views continue to dominate most biologists and psychologists, dictating a model of organisms that seems outmoded even by the rigorous standards of physics itself. Simply stated, the foundation uniting these various frameworks is that nature is inert, that gross visible matter is ultimate, that matter and consciousness are irrevocably sundered—or, alternatively, that conciousness is nothing in its own right and can be reduced to and explained solely through the laws of matter; life and mind being "nothing but" combinations of inert atoms, random and isolated from all other atoms. Such a theory may be logically consistent and brilliantly argued, as in the case of Hume, its most articulate 18th-century representative, and Jacques Monod, his 20th-century heir. These thinkers maintain that the complex world of organisms is built up from "the outside in," as it were, through accretions of matter and its eventual adaptation to the environment, in a process characterized by Darwin as "the survival of the fittest," and by Monod (1970) as "chance and necessity." The corollary to those views is that consciousness—including the artistic, philosophical, and religious capacities of man—is nothing but the consequence of the organization of matter and motion, animated at most by a vital thrust. No purpose but survival ultimately informs these particles, and to claim special privileges for consciousness is to commit the arch-sin of empiricist–positivistic philosophies: violation of the Principle of Parsimony known as Occam's Razor, which states that multiplying one's hypothesis beyond need is illegitimate. An example of violating Occam's Razor in connection with healing is sometimes invoked by overzealous and narrow-minded critics who claim that recourse to a universal healing power is akin to explaining the workings of a car by postulating a redundant little man or a nature spirit sitting inside the hood. To refute such a charge is difficult and may at present be impossible. One can, however, counter its narrowness and challenge the validity of the analogy with the observation that such an argument may well beg the question—a fallacy that violates the laws of logic and is thus far more serious than an alleged violation of the Principle of Parsimony.

While scientific validation of the Healing Hypothesis remains an abiding goal that constitutes a challenge, we must be aware that we are dealing with a domain in which too rigid a form of the positivist–physicalist model of proof may not be appropriate. New paradigms of proof and explanation may have to be evolved, combining rigor of mind with intuitive sensitivity to subtler realms of being. An unquestioning adherence at the outset to materialistic frameworks and assumptions about the nature of reality will tend to bar its adherents from investigating any other forms of healing, be this Therapeutic Touch, laying-on of hands, or distant healing. The reason for this is both basic and consistent, as we shall see below when we contrast this orientation with that of the nonreductionistic camp. First, however, let us sketch a few of the philosophical and theoretical frameworks built upon the foundation just outlined.

Reductionistic Philosophies

Among the frameworks built on the reductionistic foundation are the philosophies of Bacon, Hobbes, Descartes, and Hume. Since Descartes (1641), in particular, constructed a model of man and nature in the 17th century that our contemporary culture still implicitly accepts, we shall have to pay special attention to his outlook. The Cartesian universe is dualistic and thus incompatible with the holistic foundation that underlies all theories of healing. If Descartes' metaphysics is correct, there can be no such thing as spiritual healing. His insistence on a rigid disjunction between consciousness and matter produces the mind-body dualism which Descartes bequeathed to subsequent philosophy and psychology. Consciousness and matter (or thought and extension) are two distinct and irreducible kinds of substance, differing not only in degrees but in kind. Each has attributes not shared by the other. Matter is physical, extended (in space), visible, divisible, subject to scientific description, and quantifiable. It is lifeless, blind, inert, and acted upon by external mechanical forces.

By contrast, consciousness is nonmaterial, invisible, nonextended, indivisible, alive; its essence, its very being, is self-awareness, intentionality, and purposiveness, as Descartes proves in his immortal phrase: "I think, therefore I am" (*Cogito, ergo sum*). The consequences of Descartes' analysis, particularly as it concerns human beings, is that it irrevocably sunders man and nature, mind and body, life and the lifeless, into distinct domains. Having once sundered these, Descartes cannot get them back together. Indeed, he cannot even account for their interaction and hence is forced to espouse the view that no two substances so totally distinct can possibly interact. The unfortunate by-product of such dualism is the divorcement of man and nature, subject and object, inner and outer, consciousness and matter, leading (for reasons too complex to pursue in the present discussion) to the dissociation bordering on conceptual schizophrenia from which our culture suffers to this day. Alarmed by his own position, Descartes tried to remedy these drastic effects by offering in *Meditation VI* (1641) the hypothesis of mind–body interaction via the pineal gland in the midbrain, where presumably mind and body do interact. But this was of no help in erasing his dichotomy, and his theory was rejected as inconsistent and untenable by Spinoza (1677).

Not only did the Cartesian legacy burden us with an untenable and schizophrenic metaphysics; it paved the way for an ethics of exploitation and ruthless indifference toward the natural world. To take but one example, Descartes (1649) regarded animals as "automata," bundles of matter governed entirely by mechanical forces. Although he granted them sensation and even life, which "I regard...as consisting simply in the heat of the heart," Descartes (1649) writes that his view "is not so much cruel to animals as indulgent to men...since it absolves them from the suspicion of crime when they eat or kill animals." His judgment of animals as "natural automata" seems to have been based largely on their lack of speech, which to Descartes signified absence of thought and hence of a soul, a conclusion virtually dictated by his theology. Such reasoning is instructive as an example of the excesses to which a misguided metaphysics can lead, especially when coupled with self-righteous rationalization, as seems to have been the case with Descartes, who in other matters ranked with the best thinkers of his century.

In this as in other views, it is easy to trace a continuity between Descartes and our own time. Quite aside from the fact that the theory outlined above provides a good conscience for much current animal experimentation whose callousness few of us can face, it can also be argued that man's recklessness in robbing nature of her resources has its roots in that selfsame misguided metaphysics. Man is the thinker, the conscious being who has dominion over a dead and unconscious world of matter and over unfeeling brutes. These entities are little more than matter that moves, and that moves, moreover, in tune to man, the only self-conscious piper in the universe apart from God, who first announced man's rule over animals in Genesis. The interaction between man and the rest of creation in Descartes is thus the interaction between an alive and purposeful entity and an inert domain of dull and clodlike matter awaiting man's orders and dancing to his tune. Such a view is utterly alien to that of a healing and holistic cosmos.

Cartesian Consciousness

A second consequence of Cartesian metaphysics that directly bears on the Healing Hypothesis is Descartes' treatment of the self. One result of *Meditation II*, in which Descartes constructs his renowned *cogito*, is that only I myself can have access to consciousness. I can know myself to be conscious and thus know that "I am I" only during such times as I actively attend to my identity. Better yet, I can fully know it only in the process of thinking or saying it. Descartes (1641) spells this out clearly, unaware of the consequences to which his conclusion was to lead: "I must finally conclude and maintain that this proposition: *I am, I exist*, is necessarily true every time that I pronounce it or conceive it in my mind." It is a prescription of alienation from others, for if Descartes' conclusion is correct, how can I know that other human beings are conscious beings like myself? Clearly, I cannot know it, since I have no direct access to the consciousness of another, but only to my own. Thus, I cannot prove that other people are conscious at all. They might, like animals, be automata, and according to Descartes, I can at best infer their self-conscious humanity, in a conjecture that can never yield certainty. With this reasoning, Descartes introduces into philosophy one of its most hopeless impasses, which contemporary philosophy has termed "the problem of the Other" and which to this day it has little prospect of resolving. Insofar as empirical evidence is concerned, "the Other" is an alien being. My only certitude concerning him remains restricted to him as a bundle of matter, and in fact to a limited aspect of this, namely extension (*res extensa*). With respect to his so-called consciousness, mind, spirit, soul, will, feelings, intentions, etc., I can have no direct and consequently no reliable evidence, a situation giving rise to the solipsistic dilemma to which Descartes' outlook directly leads. Solipsism is a philosophical position asserting that, since I can prove only my own existence, all the rest of the universe including human beings may well be an illusion, a dream, or a delusion inspired by Descartes' diabolical "malevolent genius" who is bent on deceiving us.

I have dwelled on these two features—Descartes' mind–body dualism and man's isolation from nature and from fellow men via Cartesian solipsism—because they bring out most sharply the fundamentals not only of Descartes' own framework but also its persistent stranglehold on the thought of our time. To cite a most obvious example, let us take the case of behaviorism, the dominant outlook of contemporary biology and psychology, and particularly the theories of B. F. Skinner, in whom the Cartesian outlook has continued with only certain modifications (which are irrelevant to the Healing Hypothesis and thus lie beyond the scope of this chapter).

Skinner (1948) implicitly accepts the Cartesian framework, departing from it significantly in one respect, namely in his views on consciousness and self-consciousness. While Descartes still insists that my own self-consciousness (my immediate awareness of an *I* "in here") is both primary and irreducible, Skinner rejects this latter claim as unfounded metaphysics and mysticism. Only principles of matter, operating through conditioning, his "science of behavior," need be invoked in explaining human consciousness, from its most simplified to its subtlest forms. Thus, Skinner repudiates Descartes' dualism of matter and consciousness each as a basic, primary reality, and with it the distinction between brain and mind. For Skinner, whether we deal with animals or with man, matter is the only variable needed to account for behavior. There is no "mind" in addition to a brain, utilizing the latter for its purposes, as will be claimed by the frameworks we shall examine later. For Skinner, the idea of a "mind" or "consciousness" is a misnomer, a fictitious, abstract and nonmaterial entity that has no place in his reductionist ontology, in which the entire universe and all its happenings can be satisfactorily explained by invoking matter alone. All other explanatory principles are abandoned as both superfluous and illusory.

Surveying and summarizing the frameworks which rest on foundations that conflict with the Healing Hypothesis, we need but review the major premises of the Cartesian–Skinnerian outlook. No spiritual healing can exist in a universe constructed according to these views, for the Healing Hypothesis, as stated at the outset, totally rejects that foundation in favor of one differing from it in both structure and function.

Holistic Foundations

Turning away from that foundation, we can discern some basic principles that, by contrast with the above-stated ones, do not conflict with but are philosophically compatible with healing, furnishing a theoretical foundation for the Healing Hypothesis.

The most fundamental of these principles is the claim that there is but one reality. This strict nondualistic basis for the entire cosmos is the starting point for any explanation of healing. It postulates an organic unity beneath the multiplicity evident to our senses, a unity that is primary and causal compared with the derivative and secondary status of the manifested things in the world (i.e., the objects of our sense perceptions) (Kunz, 1963). That being the case, matter and consciousness are but two expressions of the one unbroken reality. They differ at best in degree and in function but not in kind. On the surface, this position may also sound reductionistic and hence reminiscent of the very behaviorism rejected earlier in this discussion. In fact, the present view is diametrically distinct from the Cartesian–Skinnerian one, since the interconnected oneness proclaimed here is a living force that unites all beings through integration, not reduction (Weber, 1975). Any apparent "reductionism" found here favors consciousness as the primary nature of reality, a consciousness in which the universe becomes unified. Consciousness thus is no incidental factor, an "epiphenomenon" or by-product as in Skinner, but an integral feature of being (Koestler and Smythies, 1969). The cosmos is alive throughout, from the lowliest atom to the highest human (or even meta-human) manifestations. Life is a continuum, expressing in endlessly diverse dimensions the inner pulse that gave it impetus toward outer manifestation. "Consciousness" may have different meanings at different levels and in the various orders of being, but this is due to diversity in complexity and organization, and in the subtlety of its substance. Beneath all life beats a unified rhythm, interconnecting every being as an expression of the same conscious, nonmaterial reality (Kunz, 1963).

Matter and energy are equivalent, two interchangeable facets of one ground, as Einstein, echoing the ancient metaphysics, was to assert in our own era. The universe, far from being a machine or composed of atomistic, separate, and random particles as alleged by physicalism, is in fact one integral whole in which the parts— actually interconnected deep within this ocean of oneness—all bear directly on one another, exerting mutual influence and interdependence in all directions and dimensions, as is the case with any living organism. These contrasting claims form two prototypically distinct frameworks: the Platonic and that of Skinner (which latter also may be said to represent theorists like Hobbes and Hume). Plato, in *Timaeus*, describes the universe as a living organism, "endowed with intelligence and a soul," which "God fashioned...by form and number," and whose "body was harmonized by proportion." Skinner (1948), by contrast, depicts nature as an alien realm that must be conquered ("Triumph over nature"), and the most recurrent word in *Walden Two*, his blueprint for a future utopia, is "control," wielded over the natural world by technocrats intent on a single goal: the satisfaction of their desires.

Conflicting Anatomies of Reality

The single most significant feature of these contrasting accounts revolves around the issue of purposiveness, intelligence, and vision imputed to the universe, or rather to its underlying spiritual reality by Eastern and Platonic philosophy, by contrast to the haphazard, blind, value-free events attributed to it by the various mechanistic versions. As in the case of other features claimed by the latter, if the mechanistic characterization of reality were correct, spiritual healing would have no legitimate foundation and would thus be impossible: an illusion due to a crass so-called placebo effect. Those engaged in it would be self-deluded at best, fraudulent at worst. (The "placebo effect," itself a complex and poorly understood phenomenon that may well be related to healing, lies beyond the scope of my discussion.)

Thus, the question as to the kind of cosmos in which we live is crucial to our assessment of the healing phenomenon. The mechanistic–materialistic–behavioristic hypothesis renders spiritual healing impossible on *a priori* grounds, for as has been pointed out, it is inconsistent with the very nature of the universe in which those systems claim we live. If, on the contrary, the holistic–spiritual–vitalistic thesis is right, the Healing Hypothesis is vastly strengthened. It even becomes a natural outgrowth of such a metaphysics, expressing in empirical ways a network of forces embodying the principles whose existence those systems assert. In this view, healing is a natural, not supernatural, consequence of the anatomy of the universe.

The purposiveness or teleological tenor of the latter account of reality also entails certain subsidiary principles. Among these are the view that the dynamism quite naturally associated with living systems rules out static passivity or inertness on the part of any being in the universe. Such a dynamic and stirring sea of energy, pushing from within (Kunz, 1963) towards ever-greater growth and self-awareness is most aptly grasped in terms of evolution, a spiritually motivated thrust at all levels of existence that culminates in an increasingly self-conscious cosmos, akin to Teilhard de Chardin's *omega point* (1959), or to the liberation of spirit slumbering within matter that has become self-transparent. This last idea is widely shared in the philosophies and religions of India, in the ancient systems of Egypt and Greece, and in theosophical concepts embodied in the esoteric tradition of both East and West (Weber, 1975). Consciousness, in short, is world-creating.

These accounts—Sankhya-Yogic, Buddhist, Pythagorean, and Platonic, to name but a few—all agree on some basic assertions. Consciousness, being primary, conceives, constructs, and subsequently governs gross visible matter, including the physical body. Since the world works "from within without" (according to the ancient Hermetic principle), from the hidden spiritual domain outward toward the dense manifest material ones, consciousness "makes itself a body," as it were. Far from being subject to gross matter, consciousness is in every way its sovereign (Smith, 1975). Since consciousness is one at its source (Schrödinger, 1969) and is the root of the cosmic reality, consciousness at some deeper level is in direct and immediate contact both with itself, as humanity, and with its ground, the infinite source. This ancient claim has gained unexpected support in the recent work of London theoretical physicist David Bohm (1978), whose distinction between the implicate–explicate orders, or the manifest–nonmanifest domains, lends further credibility to the foundation under present discussion. If it is correct, Cartesian solipsism is an empirical as well as a logical error, an absurdity which belies and contradicts the way things really are, namely, the universal unity of being. To explain it briefly, the *implicate order* postulated by Bohm (1980) asserts that all entities in the universe are *enfolded* within one another and therefore in direct touch. Their alleged separation holds true in the *unfolded* or *explicate* order, where the testimony of our senses can be taken seriously and trusted only up to a point, for the senses provide us with a clue about the deeper realities that lie beyond their grasp. Recent physics, notably quantum mechanics, makes clear that the explicate or unfolded order of nature is not the only one, and is in fact our most limited and incoherent perspective. Bohm maintains that only the postulation of an implicate, ultimately unbroken order of nature can provide a coherent and clear account of the findings of twentieth-century physics, as well as account for the workings of consciousness.

Holistic Frameworks

In all these theories, and at the farthest extreme of solipsism, we find a model in which all entities are intimately in touch with and influenced by one another, attuned to the rhythms flowing through each and through the whole. In addition to interconnectedness, a second feature of this unity is its order. The universe tends naturally toward order, as Pythagoras and Plato observed some 25 centuries ago. In spite of surface manifestations to the contrary (earthquakes and other cataclysmic events), even the most pessimistic account of nature would have to concede the overwhelming preponderance of orderly processes without which the profusion of thriving species governed by laws would not be in evidence today. Such an observation, to take an historical example, struck Plato so forcefully that he postulated an entire cosmos pervaded by purposiveness, i.e., a teleological universe (*telos* is the Greek word for "purpose, aim").

The telos of the entire universe is the expression of a spiritual force Plato termed "the good," which disposed all things toward their own maximum well-being and provided a kind of cosmic model or blueprint toward which everything "aspires" or strives. This model, Plato's Forms, might be termed an invisible DNA or RNA on a cosmic scale. Like the miniaturized models invoked by contemporary genetics, Plato's Forms are characterized by their capacity to impart order and intelligence to nature. They are the blueprints for the outer expression of the inner essence of things. Plato's philosophy thus has a natural affinity with healing theories. In both, the primary and natural state of entities is order and wholeness, linked by a rhythm attuning each entity to the rhythm of the universe, with salutary effects on the participants in the cosmic dance, reminiscent of the "dance of Shiva" in Hindu cosmology.

The Primacy of the Abstract

A contemporary scientific complement to this view, touched on above, is the holographic model of reality independently proposed by Bohm (1978) and by Stanford neuropsychologist Karl Pribram (1971, 1976, 1979). It states that in-phase experiencing of this rhythm is perceived by us as flow, joy, spontaneity, insight and intuition, intrinsic kinship with and hence compassion for all that lives. The attendant sense of well-being might even be taken as an ideal state of health for organisms, since it is derived from their harmony with the whole. Experience out-of-phase with the holomovement, on the other hand, blocks those positive and health-giving rhythms and in their stead substitutes dysrhythmias, leading to disease, a term that holistic theories deem synonymous with disorder.

Consequently, the Holistic Hypothesis postulates as the primary cause of disease the disconnectedness from this flow and rhythm of the whole, both within the single organism and also among groups of organisms. Lest one conclude that such postulation is simple (or even simplistic), I must add that the actual causes for the dysrhythmias are complex and multiple. They seem subtly interwoven with many secondary and contributory factors (genetic, environmental, etc.), which given the primitive state of our knowledge concerning these matters, we can at present only partly understand. Among such factors are our emotions, habits, energy expenditures, and values—patterns all capable of either squandering or preserving our organismic integrity. Additional variables are life-styles, involving dietary or other excesses, and even antecedent conditions both recent and remote, known in Eastern philosophy as *karma*. Through any one or, as seems likely, through a combination of these, the organism ruptures the rhythms prescribed by its proper blueprint, adversely affecting the *chakras* (Leadbeater, 1927; Powell, 1969) within the subtle energy fields which basically govern our health. Malfunctioning of the chakras eventually becomes organic malfunction.

The theory of subtle energy fields is indispensable and constitutes a crucial foundation for the Healing Hypothesis. The two frameworks in which this foundation is most explicitly elaborated are the Sankhya of classical Hindu philosophy and the Platonic cosmology of Greece. Since these are intricate and technical systems, here I can provide at best a glimpse into them. Sankhya and Plato are bound together by a common premise: the primacy of the abstract. This proclaims that invisible realities precede and in fact beget visible ones. Differently phrased, this principle reappears in contemporary physics: subtler states of matter are more primary than gross physical ones, both in order of appearance and in sovereignty over the denser forms (Bohm, 1978). This ancient conception turns commonsense naive realism (i.e., "seeing is believing") upside down. It substitutes in its stead an account of the world expressed most perfectly in Greek and Indian Idealism and in the visionary physics of David Bohm's holomovement. Their basic thesis is that a spiritual reality underlies and gives rise to our physical one, which it also sustains and governs through universal laws. In Plato, this ultimate reality is termed "the good," an undefinable force that pervades the cosmos and can account for its most minute workings by means of a more proximate, also nonmaterial principle, namely the Forms. Embedded in and generated by the Platonic Forms are the archetypal, nonphysical blueprints alluded to earlier in this discussion. Their status has puzzled scholars for over two thousand years. Somehow they seem to constitute the key to the existence and functioning of the multiplicity of physical entities in our visible world.

Platonic Philosophy

Without entering into the philosophical complexities of Plato's Theory, its noteworthy feature for our purposes can be summed up quite simply: the existence and nature of any given entity depends upon its correctly reproducing the eternal, essential Platonic Form in whose "image" it is made. In the case of living organisms, for example, proper "participation" (*methexis*, in Greek) in the Form translates into health, whereas faulty participation leads to illness. "Health" in Plato involves the spiritual well-being of the whole person.

The applicability of such a view to healing is evident, although its detailed workings-out are exceedingly difficult and subtle. However, the direction dictated by this theory falls quite easily into such healing principles as we presently possess, even at this rudimentary juncture in the state of the art. Plato assigns the primary power for health or illness not to the visible outgrowth, the consequence of the archetype in flesh, blood, and other matter, as is the claim of the materialists or of commonsense naive realists. In a bold inversion of causal connections, he instead attributes well-being to our unobstructed connectedness with the Forms in such a way that we can "translate" their patterns, first into the invisible, subtler "bodies" or energy fields, and subsequently into the gross visible, denser, and stabler forms of matter of which our physical bodies are composed. As in Bohm's implicate–explicate orders (1978), for Plato it is our relationship to these supersensible realities that determines proper functioning. This is not the place to present the many details that lie scattered throughout the Platonic dialogues and that can be woven together into a coherent theory of health and healing. However, anyone embarked (as the writer currently is) on such an enterprise gains increasing conviction that a Platonic theory of healing exists embedded in the opus as a whole, even though it must be carefully culled therefrom and made explicit.

The second and more important point is that Plato, even were he never to mention human health or disease, furnishes an indirect framework for the Healing Hypothesis through his metaphysics as a whole. Reduced to its barest outline, Platonic metaphysics postulates an ideal, eternal, supersensible model, beyond space and time, and a material, spatiotemporal counterpart which without the archetypal supersensible entity cannot continue to be, let alone to flourish. To be hale and whole is therefore impossible without continuing interaction with the eternal and higher-dimensional realm, Plato's ideal, intelligible world. In that sense, it may rightfully be argued that lack of health is lack of wholeness, i.e. partiality, undue restrictedness, isolation from the cosmic matrix, and self-enclosure, diminishing the dynamic balance in which healthy entities exist, by cutting off their ontological circulation, as it were. This state of affairs is nowhere more powerfully presented than in Plato's Allegory of the Cave (*Republic* VII), where partiality and physicalism are equated with an imprisoned state of blindness, curable by the abandonment of the cave for the realm of light which alone can set man free and make him flourish.

One might sum up Plato's philosophy with the observation that Platonic metaphysics as a whole is a model for healing.

Indian Philosophy

The second metaphysical framework especially appropriate here is the Sankhya of sixth century B.C. India. In some ways it may be even more suitable to healing theories than the Platonic one because it deals more extensively with biological organisms. These are the direct expression of Spirit (*purusha*) becoming unaccountably entangled with root-matter (*prakriti*), leading through a series of complex but plausible steps to cosmic consciousness (*mahat*). This field-like force ultimately localizes itself into an individuating capacity which provides the potential for self-consciousness, the "I-making" capacity (*ahamkāra*). One manifestation of this personal focusing of universal consciousness is mind (*manas*) or mental field, an active energy that can be understood only teleologically, not mechanistically as in behavioristic accounts. The alleged dualism of *Sankhya*, mind or intelligence is the impetus for generating the physical, emotional, and vital (etheric) energy fields by which individual self-consciousness ("personality," as we call it) expresses itself in the phenomenal–empirical space–time world. Mind, and ultimately spiritual consciousness, makes matter by precipitating itself, as it were, into dense and stable forms of substance. As in Plato, mind governs matter, a hierarchy or metaphysical "pecking-order" that seems attributable to its greater energy. In this lies its tremendous power, for good or for ill, to affect the destiny of the physical field, since an atom of subtler matter contains more energy, more wholeness and hence more power than one of dense physical matter (Kunz, 1977; Bohm, 1978).

Although this highly telescopic précis can do no more than evoke these bold and intriguing speculations, their implications can be spelled out, even if their richly elaborated details cannot in a paper so limited in scope. These implications lead to a sweeping yet minutely refined cosmology in which all beings fit into the interconnected whole adverted to elsewhere in this essay. This schema overlaps, as we have seen, with parts of our own scientific account, even though its metaphysical postulations would be unacceptable to science in its present state. To summarize the claims of *Sankhya*: individual consciousness produces the structures necessary to its evolution in the world from the potential "elements" or abstract, nonmaterial genetic "seeds." These give rise, through a process of "condensation," to forms of increasingly gross physical matter, from atoms to molecules (*shtulabhutāni*, literally "dense material particles"), which in turn behave such as do the molecules described by contemporary Western science. Molecules ultimately form organic compounds, and these evolve to become plant and finally animal organisms, culminating in self-conscious beings like man (and in meta-human manifestations of consciousness). The convergence of *Sankhya* with contemporary Western science occurs therefore at the later stages of explanation of this process; a sharp divergence exists with respect to both the initial stages and the teleological tone of the *Sankhya* system, for Western science does not at present accept the idea of consciousness as the catalyst for the origin, development, and rationale of the physical world, nor for that matter the deeper purposive and holistic context in which *Sankhya* lies anchored.

It may be asked: what practical differences do the explanations presented thus far entail, and more specifically: what are their consequences for healing? We shall see that insofar as both the possibility and the practice of healing are concerned, drastic practical differences do arise from such divergent views. In materialistic-

physicalist philosophies, both functions and malfunctions are attributable to the workings of gross physical matter without recourse to
consciousness. This observation still holds, even though the view is
being increasingly eroded within the medical community itself,
through the compelling experience of every medical practitioner
that mind and emotions play a central role in so-called psychosomatic and perhaps in all diseases. However that may be, no good
theoretical ground presently exists to deal with such findings. In
our current transitional stage, the physician attempts to integrate
the psychosomatic reality with which his clinical experience daily
confronts him, into the physicalism that remains to this day the
preeminent metaphysics of medicine. Treating the whole person
still lies in the future.

By contrast, as we have seen, holistic philosophies attribute
the primary power of both health and disease to consciousness, not
to its material consequences within the gross physical field, i.e., to
the manifestations of consciousness. We must of course realize that
even the divisions I have pursued here are artificial ones which the
spiritual traditions repudiate. We may discern differences at the
phenomenal level between so-called matter and consciousness, but
at their root they are one—parallel expressions of the indivisible
and single reality that secures their foundation (Govinda, 1969).

The Yoga of Patānjali

Such an outlook invites a nondualistic orientation in both theory
and practice. By way of example, the *Yoga Sūtras of Patānjali*, the
classical treatise on physiology and psychology built upon Sankhya
theory, makes some penetrating clinical and therapeutic observations directly applicable to healing. I refer to Patānjali's theory of
the *samskāras* or scars, which he claims play a prominent role in
health and disease (Kunz, 1976, 1977, 1978, 1979; Taimni, 1975).
These scars are tracings left on us by our experience, akin to
energy patterns etched into our organism. Perhaps this occurs at
the cellular, neuronal, or even deeper levels, preserving, by en-
coding, what have been termed engrams of energy, i.e., records of

experience that become part and parcel of our very tissues. In ways not yet understood by modern neurophysiology nor sufficiently explained by Patānjali, these "furrows" or tracings persist throughout our lives, exercising enormous influence on our behavior by their very presence. Their influence on our energy economy is for the most part destructive and maladaptive, in that traumas and disappointments rather than joyful and fulfilling experiences are retained and energized to our detriment, much as Freud and the 20th-century analytic schools have argued in their theories of an unconscious that dominates us. Since Patānjali, like the psychoanalytic therapists, was impressed by the widespread power and tenacity of these "scars," wreaking havoc with the entire psychosomatic edifice, his approach to their dissolution is radical and holistic rather than a piecemeal strategy, which he rejects as useless in coping with the roots and not the mere branches of the conflict.

Accordingly, Patānjali's advice for defusing and deenergizing their destructive effect falls under what today we would call a healing approach. He observes that mere verbal techniques—reasoning with the traumatic tracings or willing oneself to ignore their presence—are powerless in the face of the vitality with which the scars are endowed. If anything, such tactics tend to sustain them with renewed energy, by focusing on and thus continually reinforcing the tracings through a negative energy pattern. Patānjali urges "starving" them at their root, withering their structure and leaving in their place an "extinct" and harmless scar sapped of its force and thus of its power to damage our lives.

This withdrawal of energy can come about in a variety of ways, some of them almost contemporary in their coherence, for example, with the approach of Simonton and co-workers (1978) to stress diseases and cancer therapy, and the work of Achterberg and colleagues (1976) derived from it. Patānjali specifically advocates visualization. This operates through identification with certain catalytic images on which we meditate. Most powerful in rebalancing our energies are yoga and meditation, which are Patānjali's analogues to healing. Yoga, i.e., union, rejoins the part with the cosmic whole. In its highest expression, the culmination of the process known as *samadhi*, yoga actually integrates man into the universal healing power whose orderliness sweeps away the scars. Obliterating psychophysical lesions by its very presence and power, it seems to *overwhelm* the dysrhythmic patterns in favor of the health-giving rhythmic ones that wipe them out. Thus yoga, in the far-reaching sense envisioned by Patānjali, radically alters our pathological patterns by erasing, as it were, the garbled and twisted records furrowed within our energy-fields (Kunz, 1976, 1977, 1978, 1979).

Patānjali's outlook finds echoes in Western philosophies widely separated from him in space, time, and culture, where no direct historical influence can be demonstrated. There is, for example, a coherence of vision linking him with Pythagoras (sixth century B.C.), who precedes him by at least four centuries. The father of psychosomatic medicine in the West, Pythagoras prescribed music to restore the imbalanced frame to its rightful balance, "rightful" because Pythagoras taught that an unheard cosmic rhythm, the "music of the spheres," pervades the universe, undetected by us only due to the high velocity of its vibration, approaching the speed of light. This "music," composed of ratio, pattern, harmony, and mathematical proportion, as Pythagoras held, orders the life of both nature and man, whose intrinsic unity is proclaimed as the isomorphism of macrocosm and microcosm, the Hermetic dictum: "as above, so below." Man is but a finite mirror of the universe as a whole. A diseased organism has lost its harmonic character to the discordant rhythms already referred to, and hence Pythagorean therapy aims at restoring the proper harmonics and "musical" patterns to the patient's life field. Plato, Pythagoras' greatest disciple, concurs with these concepts and draws on them in his theory of organismic and social justice in *The Republic*, where harmonics becomes the key to both health and wisdom.

Spinoza

In the modern era of Western philosophy, the healing framework is powerfully revived by Spinoza, the 17th-century rationalist whose philosophy seeks to combat the dualism and general fragmentation of his predecessor, Descartes. Mind and body are not two distinct substances but two ways of describing one and the same spiritual substance which Spinoza (1677) terms God or Nature. To

Spinoza, the insoluble Cartesian dilemma of mind–body interaction is a pseudo-problem, nothing more than conceptual and linguistic confusion bred by a misunderstanding of the nature of things. The metaphysical ground of our being is one, the seamless garment of nature expressing itself both as consciousness and as matter, the two attributes (out of the infinitely many) that can be known by man. It follows from Spinoza's premises that disorder in any part of our organism involves concomitant disorder in all of it, since the cosmic ecology is a single fabric. A healthy consciousness is reflected in a healthy body; the converse connection is equally valid. No interaction, no "influence," and no causal account is warranted or needed since all these falsely assume the separation of a unity which Spinoza sees as the primary fact of life. Along with Parmenides (fifth century B.C. Greece), he is the most thoroughgoing and radical monist within the Western tradition, holding tenaciously to his view despite the testimony of the senses which encourages conclusions to the contrary.

Moreover, Spinoza's denial of dualism furnishes the basis of a remarkably modern physiology and psychology, set forth in his great treatise *Ethic* (Parts III, IV, V). In a theory that may well turn out to be prophetic—cohering with holographic concepts of modern physics and neurology mentioned earlier in this chapter—Spinoza observes, for example, that negative emotions and thoughts damage the organism, leading not only to despair and depression but, as his monism requires, to physical deterioration as well. Specifically, Spinoza singles out such affects as hatred, fear, jealousy, envy, guilt, regret, pity, self-pity, ruminative and self-centered obsessive thinking, dwelling on real or imagined injuries received from others—all of them destructive to our health. His concept of the *conatus*, a psychophysiological energy reminiscent of *prana* in Indian systems, cuts across all aspects of our constitution. A heightened *conatus* spells well-being, harmony with the cosmic flow whose presence we register as "joy" or "blessedness," the highest happiness human beings can experience. Spinoza tells us that compassion, affection, contemplation of the laws of the universe leading to a grasp of its grandeur—that all these heighten the vital energy (*conatus*) which holds the key to our health.

Accordingly Spinoza, like Pythagoras, Plato, Patañjali, Buddha, and others within this tradition, counsels a life of measure and moderation, characterized by altruism, optimism, joyful participation in the cosmic order facilitated by, but also in turn reinforcing, a selfless and saintly life of simple happiness.

Many of these foregoing views—dormant during the long centuries in which atomistic, materialistic, or dualistic hypothesis gained ascendancy in the scientific community—are now being revived within science itself. Most notable amidst these attempts is the holographic paradigm propounded by Bohm and Pribram. The holomovement, to use Bohm's term, is a spiritual, dynamic, unbroken reality in which all entities are embedded and interconnected. Although its full nature is inaccessible to our discursive mind, we can intuit its presence, particularly in meditative awareness, which may be described as a unitive, healing, direct experience of it. All our concepts concerning it are metaphorical, for the "ocean of energy" in which we are immersed lies beyond language. It can be apprehended, but not comprehended (Bohm, 1978).

The Role of the Healer

I have tried to present some highlights of philosophical frameworks hospitable to the Healing Hypothesis. The remaining task of this chapter is to consider the role of the healer himself. From the discussion thus far, we may conclude that his role is at once modest and powerful. Since consciousness has been accorded a creative status in the scheme of things, its role is that of an active energy capable of balancing the gross physical and even the subtler realms of matter. This premise is required by the Healing Hypothesis, which holds that a consciously focused intent is a force rather than a fantasy. That force influences all dimensions of "matter," be they physical, etheric, emotional, mental, or spiritual, since all of these overlap in any event. The healer's intent forms an energy capable of affecting the disturbed patterns of the healee. We must, however, be clear on the crucial issue. The universal healing power, not the healer's personal energy, accomplishes the healing. The healer is akin to a channel, passively, yet paradoxically with discernment, permitting the cosmic energy to flow unobstructedly through his own fields into those of the healee. He must be sensitive to the disturbances within the healee and simultaneously aware of the healee's wholeness at higher levels of being, an art that demands both discrimination and intuition. In short, the healer constitutes the link between the universal and the particular, analogous to an electrical transformer capable of stepping down the source, in this case the prodigious cosmic energy, into a form utilizable by our systems. But it must be emphasized that this is neither a mechanical nor an automatic process. The healer's intentionality—his desire to help and his compassion for the suffering Other—is a necessary but not a sufficient condition for contact with the healing source. The sufficient condition (i.e., the factor in whose presence healing cannot fail to take place) remains largely a mystery at present.

A number of factors have been proposed in the attempt to probe its workings. Among these are individual susceptibility to the healing energy as well as differences in our capacity to give up fundamental and familiar energy patterns, overcoming the natural tendency to cling to their miscoded information through fear of change. Finally, the decisive factor may be an ideal synchronicity of all three fields: infinite source, healer, and healee. About this, the most interesting theory of all, we know very little as yet. Such synchronicity implies a "time" quite different from Newtonian or clock time. The suspension of clock time in favor of atemporality—the eternal moment—seems a basic part of the healing framework. It can account for the well-documented albeit rare cases of instantaneous and complete healing in certain individuals, apparently a sweeping restructuring and reintegration of all their energy fields amounting, in addition to a physical cure, to a total transformation of the personality and its values (Kunz, 1977, 1978). In such an event, the pathological physical patterns are erased and realigned with their etheric and subtler fields much like the erasure of a distorted tape recording and its replacement by orderly instruction and information. In the absence of such ideal synchronicity, where the healing energy can only partly break through the disordered patterns (which tend to block its natural flow and dilute its impact), there seems to be partial and less dramatic restoration, less lasting because the patient's disturbed rhythms tend to reassert themselves, eventually repatterning the physical fields along the old "grooves" which led to the disease in the first place (Kunz, 1978; Meek, 1977; Tiller, 1975, 1977). The person is potentially but not actually whole. Lastly, our self-image bears crucially on our capacity to both heal and be healed.

As even this most cursory discussion has established, healing is a complex pattern of interactions between three unbounded fields of energy: the infinite source, the healer, and the healee. The latter two can, incidentally, often exchange roles, each guiding the other to seek renewed instruction from the source. This leads to the inference that the healer serves to speed up the healee's own innate capacity to contact the archetypal blueprint, enhancing the universal tendency toward order that is part and parcel of all life (Kunz, 1976, 1978). The healer thus mediates between a finite field that has somehow "gone wrong," and the infinite ocean of energy from which we become estranged only at our peril.

Healing as Moving Meditation

The experience of union with the source is most often associated with a centered state of being in which the universal energy can pour through us without obstruction. Our thoughts, emotions, memories, anxieties—i.e., the ego and its residues—are temporarily suspended, and with it ordinary time and our confined spaces vanish. Centering ourselves in the universe as a whole rather than in any part of it, we enter a dimension beyond the limits of our daily life, an infinite or n-dimensional space–time continuum.

Paradoxically, although our consciousness has burst its empirical boundaries and flows in a vastly expanded space, we are simultaneously more unified, less fragmented, and less scattered than before. A tremendous power has gathered our energies and heightened them, focusing them as through a prism, resulting in renewed and unsuspected energy, clarity, and compassion. This state ideally favors healing, and not surprisingly all healers center themselves through some sort of meditation before proceeding to heal. This centering seems to filter out the interfering impurities spoken of earlier, and to make the healer a proper, i.e., an impersonal, channel for the universal energy, for with such impurities constitute a barrier to which it must adapt, losing some of its intensity by having to move around the obstacles.

Meditation thus conceived is an active and dynamic force in the world, not withdrawal from it to some distant cave of indifference. The healing centeredness is a mysterious combination of high energy and absolute calm. It is both active and passive, movement and stillness, purposiveness without purpose, effortless effort. In short, the act of healing is meditation in motion.

The Philosopher as Healer

The model of the healer as reconciler between the finite and infinite dimensions of reality seems to have been instinctively understood by the holistic philosophical frameworks referred to in this chapter. The metaphor of the physician-healer figures prominently in these intuitively grounded systems of both East and West. Buddha and Plato, in particular, repeatedly compare the true philosopher to the physician. The latter is no mere dispenser of medicines, manipulating molecules of matter in some sort of mechanical enterprise. The engineer, of the scientific or the "social" Skinnerian variety, who operates on levers and pulleys of a machine whose workings he conceives along mechanistic principles, though he may be of help to others, is not a healer. His mechanistic paradigm, faulty according to the Healing Hypothesis, is a symptom of fragmentation, the selfsame disorder as the disease. The physician-healer, by contrast, is the sage, conscious of the supersensible reality to which he lives attuned in thought, word, and deed. The consequent wholeness and harmony of his being make him the natural conduit for the healing energies of nature.

The Pythagorean-Platonic, Buddhist, and Spinozistic model of the philospher has intuited not only the universal harmony but also—sage that he is—gained insight into the root causes of organismic disharmony. His prescription for health involves the restoration of harmony through right living (ethics), resulting in a life of altruism enhanced by moderation and balance. In the light of this, recovery from illness entails simultaneous recovery from philosophical blindness, symbolized by Plato's Cave and by Buddha's metaphor of ignorance as a knife wound in ailing humanity's back. To be sure, partial recovery is possible, as noted, but it can bring us only a diminished state of disease. In the esoteric tradition of philosophy, restoration to total health is return to a pristine state of wholeness involving all creation and, above all, union with the ultimate source. This state is the birthright of the whole person, open to us all.

Bibliography

Achterberg, J., Simonton, O. C., and Simonton, S. *Stress, psychological factors, and cancer.* Fort Worth: New Medicine Press, 1976.

Bohm, D. *Wholeness and the implicate order.* London: Routledge, Kegan, Paul, Ltd., 1980.

Bohm, D. The Enfolding-unfolding universe. *Revision: A Journal of Knowledge and Consciousness,* 1978, *1,* 24–51.

Bohm, D. Personal communication, Ojai, Calif., April 1979.

Capra, F. *The tao of physics.* Berkeley: Shambala, 1975.

de Chardin, T. *The phenomenon of man.* New York: Harper, 1959.

Descartes, R. Meditations on first philosophy, 1641; Letter to Henry More, 1649; in *Philosophical works of Descartes.* New York: Dover Publications, 1931.

Govinda, L. *Foundations of Tibetan mysticism.* New York: Samuel Weiser, Inc., 1969.

Koestler, A., Smythies, J. R. *Beyond reductionism: new perspectives in the life of sciences.* London: Hutchinson and Co., Ltd., 1969.

Krieger, D. *The Therapeutic Touch: how to use your hands to help or to heal.* Englewood Cliffs, N.J.: Prentice-Hall, 1979.

Kunz, D. Healing Workshops. Craryville, N.Y.: 1976, 1977, 1978, 1979.

Kunz, F. L. The reality of the non-material. *Main Currents in Modern Thought,* 1963, 20, 2.

Leadbeater, C. W. *The Chakras.* Adyar, India: Theosophical Publishing House, 1927.

Meek, G. W. Toward a general theory of healing. *Healers and the healing process.* Wheaton, Ill.: Theosophical Publishing House, 1977.

Monod, J. *Le hasard et la necessité.* Paris: Editions du Seuil, 1970.

Plato. *The dialogues of Plato.* Tr. B. Jowett. New York: Random House, 1937.

Powell, A. E. *The etheric double.* Wheaton, Ill.: Theosophical Publishing House, 1969.

Pribram, K. *Languages of the brain.* Englewood Cliffs, N.J.: Prentice-Hall, 1971.

Pribram, K. Problems concerning the structure of consciousness. In G. Globus (Ed.), *Consciousness and the brain.* New York: Plenum Press, 1976.

Pribram, K. Holographic memory. An interview by Daniel Coleman in *Psychology Today,* 1979, *12,* 9.

Schrödinger, E. *What is life* and *Mind and matter.* Cambridge: Cambridge University Press, 1969.

Simonton, O. C., Simonton, S., Creighton, J. *Getting well again.* Los Angeles: J. P. Tarcher, Inc., 1978.

Skinner, B. F. *Walden two.* New York: Macmillan Publishing Co., 1948.

Smith, E. L. *Intelligence came first.* Wheaton, Ill.: Theosophical Publishing House, 1975.

Spinoza, B. Ethics (1677). In J. Wild (Ed.), *Spinoza selections.* New York: Charles Scribner's Sons, 1930.

Taimni, I. K. *The science of yoga (the yoga sutras of Patānjali).* Wheaton, Ill.: Theosophical Publishing House, 1975.

Tiller, W. *Radionics, radiesthesia, and physics.* Sausalito, Calif.: Big Sur Recordings, 1975.

Tiller, W. Theoretical modeling on the functioning of man. In G. W. Meek (Ed.), *Healers and the healing process.* Wheaton, Ill.: Theosophical Publishing House, 1977.

Weber, R. The reluctant tradition: esoteric philosophy East and West. *Main Currents in Modern Thought,* 1975, *31,* 4, 99–106.

Weber, R. The good, the true, the beautiful: are they attributes of the universe? *Main Currents in Modern Thought,* 1975, *32,* 118–125.

Weber, R. The enfolding-unfolding universe: a conversation with David Bohm. *Revision: A Journal of Knowledge and Consciousness,* 1978b, *1,* 24–51.

Chapter 3

Meditation and Therapeutic Touch

Marianne D. Borelli

The practice of laying-on of hands with the intent to help or heal goes back to ancient times. There is evidence of its use in ancient Egypt, India, and Tibet and in the writings of the Old and New Testaments. A derivative of this practice has been studied by Dolores Krieger and has been termed Therapeutic Touch. This practice is believed to involve an intentional transfer of excess body energy from a well person to one who is ill (Krieger, 1975, 1979). Therapeutic Touch has been termed "a healing meditation," by Peper and Ancoli (1979) since a meditative state of consciousness is necessary for the healer during the practice of Therapeutic Touch.

Various forms of meditation have been integral components of the religious practices of both Eastern and Western religions for centuries. Buddhists, Hindus, and Sufis in the Eastern traditions and the Christian mystics in the West have used various forms of meditation to reach their goal, whether it be liberation for the yogi or union with God for the Christian. Currently meditation is a popular practice and is being used for a variety of purposes often apart from the discipline and practice required in the classical forms of meditation. Its current uses include stress reduction and relaxation, alteration of what had previously been considered involuntary functions such as blood pressure, and as an adjunct to traditional psychotherapy (Benson, 1975; Carrington, 1977; Green and Green, 1977). While these uses are vastly different from the classical aims of meditation, they make use of the physiological and subjective states which accompany meditation and which seem to have a positive effect upon body functioning.

Meditation is related to Therapeutic Touch in two ways. First, the essential mental state of the person in the role of the healer during the process of Therapeutic Touch is a meditative state or a state of deep concentration. Those who use Therapeutic Touch exhibit an ability to attend to cues or perceptions of a more subtle nature, as is characteristic of a state of meditation. It is such cues concerning the state of the energy field of the healee which are the basis for assessment and transfer of energy during Therapeutic Touch. Second, meditation produces certain physiological responses and in so doing confronts the traditional dualism of mind and body. It confronts not only this dualism but also that of seeing man as a separate entity from all aspects of his environment. The subjective experience of meditation opens one's awareness of the basic inter-connection of the universe and of the energies inherent in it which move toward wholeness. It is upon this holistic view of mind–body–environment that Therapeutic Touch rests. This relationship between Therapeutic Touch and meditation will be more fully discussed in light of the research in both areas.

What Is Meditation?

The word *meditation* refers to a center or midst within the self. Meditation is a practice in awareness, in attunement to one's nature, in centeredness, and in the capacity of giving up oneself and being available to one's perceptions (Naranjo and Ornstein, 1971). With discipline and practice, meditation enables one to become more inner-directed and sensitive to subtler stimuli than are normally attended to in waking consciousness. Certain physiological responses also occur during meditation, the type and degree of which vary according to the experience of the meditator and the particular form of meditation used.

Naranjo and Ornstein (1971) describe two general types of meditation, one aimed at restricting awareness to an unchanging object, process, or symbol and the second aimed at the expansion of awareness of the external environment. The mode by which the state of meditation is reached is not as important as the attitude which is attained.

It is important to understand what meditation enables the individual to do. What is termed "normal" awareness is in reality a
construction process which a person has learned throughout his
particular development. At any waking moment a person is
bombarded with various types of stimuli. If all such stimuli were
attended to, sensory overstimulation and chaos would result. Instead, sensory systems filter information outside of awareness, dis-
carding that which is irrelevant or monotonous and bringing into
awareness that which serves a purpose for the individual. Models of
information which have been presented repeatedly are formed, and
stimuli related to these models are no longer attended to. In the
practice of meditation, it is the model building process which is dis-
mantled (Naranjo and Ornstein, 1971, p. 194).

When the usual means of dealing with incoming stimuli are
held in abeyance, one is able to perceive stimuli afresh and to attend to signals which were previously too weak to merit attention.
The effect of meditation has been likened to looking at the stars at
night and at noon. During the daylight hours the competing stimuli
of the sun's rays block the weaker light of the stars, making them
invisible. At night, as in the meditative state, the process of turning
off the overwhelming stimuli occurs and the stars are clearly visible.
Meditation has also been described as a process of calming the
ripples on a lake. When the lake is still, the bottom can be clearly
seen (Naranjo and Ornstein, 1971, p. 214).

Krieger (1979) describes four phases of Therapeutic Touch,
the first of which involves centering oneself, that is, finding a stable
personal reference point. Such a centered or meditative state,
which is maintained during Therapeutic Touch, can be viewed in
the context of Deikman's (1971) modes of organization of the biological and psychological dimensions of man. These two modes are
action and receptive. In the action mode, the striated muscle system and the sympathetic nervous system predominate, the EEG
shows beta waves, and the baseline muscle tension is increased. It
is a state of striving toward the achievement of goals as well as
avoiding pain. The particular attributes of this mode change
throughout the developmental interaction between the individual
and his environment, with a tendency toward sharpening perceptual and conceptual boundaries.

In contrast, the receptive mode aims at maximum intake of the environment. The sensory-perceptual system predominates rather than the striated muscle system. The EEG tends toward alpha waves, baseline muscle tension is decreased, attention is more diffuse, paralogical thought processes occur, boundary perception is decreased, and there is dominance of the sensory over the formal. In Western culture the receptive mode is more characteristic of infancy while the action mode comes into dominance during the process of growth and development.

Deikman (1971) notes that the distinction between the two modes is not comparable to activity and passivity but rather it is the goal of the organism's activity that determines the mode. He distinguishes between "letting in" environmental stimuli, which is the receptive mode and characterizes meditation, and "making it," which is the action mode.

Thus, the mental state of the healer during Therapeutic Touch is one of meditation in which information is "let in" concerning the healee. At the same time the will of the healer to effect change in the pattern and organization of the field of the healee might represent the action mode, yet it apparently cannot be accomplished without the dominance of the receptive mode. Deikman (1971, p. 487) comments that classical yogic literature and contemporary dream research suggest that paranormal phenomena require the development of the receptive mode.

Physiology of Meditation and Therapeutic Touch

The physiological responses to meditation have received much attention in the scientific community since the late sixties. Parallels can be drawn between this research and biofeedback training since both demonstrate that functions previously thought to be involuntary can be consciously altered (Green and Green, 1977).

In a study of Zen Buddhist priests before, during, and after meditation, Kasamatsu and Hirai (1973) concluded that EEG changes could be classified into four stages, which paralleled the mental state of the subject. Mental states were evaluated by the years spent in Zen training and the evaluation of a Zen master. The four stages were: (1) the appearance of alpha waves, (2) an increase in alpha amplitude, (3) a decrease in alpha frequency, and (4) the appearance of a rhythmical theta train. Only those meditators with years of practice achieved stage four. Alpha blocking was also considered with the subject's eyes open and closed. With eyes open, habituation was not recognized, but with the eyes closed habituation of alpha quickly occurred. The authors concluded that the slowing of the EEG pattern and the dehabituation of alpha blocking indicate specific changes in consciousness.

Wallace and Benson's (1972) research on practitioners of Transcendental Meditation (TM) with six months' to three years' experience indicated that this method produced many of the same effects on the autonomic nervous system that studies of Zen and yoga practitioners had shown. While meditating, subjects demonstrated what Wallace and Benson described as a "wakeful, hypometabolic state." Oxygen consumption, carbon dioxide elimination, and the rate and volume of respiration decreased. A slight increase was shown in the acidity of the arterial blood and a decrease in the blood lactate level. The pulse slowed, skin resistance increased, and the EEG showed an intensification of slow alpha waves with occasional theta wave activity. A decreased lactate level had previously been linked with a relaxed state by Pitts and McLure (1969), who found that an infusion of lactate in normal subjects could bring on a state of anxiety.

Benson (1975) describes a state that is opposite to the "fight or flight" response as termed by Cannon (1914) to signify the body's response to a perceived emergency. The Relaxation Response is achieved through the use of a meditation-like technique and is thought by Benson to occur in all forms of meditation that require a quiet body. Benson speaks of consciousness on a continuum that extends from coma to sleep, to drowsiness, to alertness, to hyperalertness. The Relaxation Response is located along this continuum and is considered to be an altered state of consciousness since it is not commonly experienced by most people. Regardless of the particular technique used, four basic elements are necessary for the Relaxation Response to occur. These are a quiet environment, an object to dwell on, a passive attitude, and a comfortable position.

The Relaxation Response produces a decreased oxygen consumption, decreased heart and respiratory rates, and a decreased arterial blood lactate level, which is indicative of decreased activity of the sympathetic nervous system. Subjectively, persons using the Relaxation Response report feeling calm and relaxed yet alert. Benson sees the Relaxation Response as a useful antidote for the stressful environment in which man lives and as a useful treatment for many stress-related diseases.

It can be seen from these studies that these forms of meditation produce certain similar physiological responses. The intensity of the response can be viewed as a continuum with novices to meditation at one end and experienced meditators at the other. While these practices are performed with the subject seated in a quiet state, other meditative techniques require strenuous movement. Correspondingly, the physiological responses of such meditators would differ in certain respects from those of Zen, Yoga, TM, and Relaxation Response practitioners.

In a pioneering study, Peper and Ancoli (1979) looked at the psychophysiological changes in healer and healee during Therapeutic Touch with Krieger as the healer. In contrast to many earlier meditation studies, which showed a predominance of alpha and theta wave activity during meditation, Krieger's EEG showed fast beta activity while performing Therapeutic Touch. EEG readings also showed that Krieger was not attending to outside cues. Peper and Ancoli concluded that these EEG changes are probably associated with Krieger's particular meditative style. It is of interest to note that during Therapeutic Touch the three patients showed an abundance of large amplitude alpha activity with eyes open and closed and reported feeling relaxed during the treatment, with no major changes in EEG, EKG, EMG (electromyograph), temperature, or GSR (galvanic skin response).

The Essential Relationship

For the person in the role of healer during Therapeutic Touch, a state of meditation during which one's attention is effortlessly focused upon the healee is a necessary condition. In the meditative state, there is an enhanced awareness of subtle cues from within the self. These cues are perceptible because the "noise" of ordinary thought processes has been temporarily suspended. Such a state is necessary for the healer during Therapeutic Touch as it enables him/her to perceive cues about the condition of the healee and about energy flow between healer and healee. Learning to listen more closely to oneself signifies a personal growth process and may initiate a journey at the end of which one is more fully human and is able to use more fully one aspect of this humanity, Therapeutic Touch.

Bibliography

Benson, H. *The relaxation response.* New York: William Morrow, 1975; Avon, 1976.

Cannon, W. B. The emergency function of the adrenal medulla in pain and the major emotions. *American Journal of Physiology,* 1914, *33,* 356–372.

Carrington, P. *Freedom in meditation.* Garden City, N.Y.: Anchor Press, 1977.

Deikman, A. Bimodal consciousness. *Archives of General Psychiatry,* 1971, *25,* 481–489.

Green, E. and Green, A. *Beyond biofeedback.* New York: Dell, 1977.

Kasamatsu, A. and Hirai, T. An electroencephalographic study of the Zen meditation (Zazen). In R. Ornstein (Ed.), *The nature of human consciousness.* San Francisco: W. H. Freeman, 1973.

Krieger, D. Therapeutic Touch: The imprimatur of nursing. *American Journal of Nursing,* 1975, *75,* 784–787.

Krieger, D. *The Therapeutic Touch: how to use your hands to help or to heal.* Englewood Cliffs, N.J.: Prentice-Hall, 1979.

Naranjo, C. and Ornstein, R. *On the psychology of meditation.* New York: Viking Press, 1971.

Peper, E. and Ancoli, S. Two endpoints of an EEG continuum of meditation—alpha/theta and fast beta. Appendix to D. Krieger, *The Therapeutic Touch: how to use your hands to help or to heal.* Englewood Cliffs, N.J.: Prentice-Hall, 1979.

Pitts, F. N. and McLure, J. The biochemistry of anxiety. *Scientific American,* 1969, *220,* 69–75.

Wallace, R. and Benson, H. The physiology of meditation. *Scientific American,* 1972, *226,* 85–86.

PART II

Current Research and Clinical Applications

In this section the reader is presented with a number of articles written by health professionals who use Therapeutic Touch. These practitioners, representing a variety of clinical areas and working with diverse populations, report on their use of Therapeutic Touch as an adjunct to conventional medical and nursing care. This section illustrates the fact that each practitioner has developed a personal concept of Therapeutic Touch and has carved out a place for its use in his/her particular setting. Although each chapter differs slightly in its approach to Therapeutic Touch, a connecting thread among the chapters becomes obvious. For these practitioners Therapeutic Touch has become a means of humanizing their interventions and in doing this they have become more sensitive and caring individuals.

Chapter 4

Therapeutic Touch: A Way of Life

Janet Macrae

The quality of mercy is not strain'd,
It droppeth as the gentle rain from heaven
Upon the place beneath: it is twice blessed;
It blesseth him that gives and him that takes.
　　　　　—The Merchant of Venice

Therapeutic Touch, a variant of the ancient laying-on of hands, is a method of healing based on an exchange of energy between healer and healee. Since professional nursing involves the act of human touch, many nurses are now using this technique as an extension of their traditional practice.

For many of us, however, Therapeutic Touch has become not only an extension of our nursing practice, but a way of life. The process requires no equipment but ourselves, so its use is not limited to the hospital setting. Wherever we are—at home, on the beach, at the grocery store—we can practice it. Furthermore, not only human beings, but all living things, will respond to Therapeutic Touch, so the opportunities for its use are innumerable.

When practicing Therapeutic Touch, we knowledgeably use ourselves to help another person regain his state of dynamic balance or integration. However, as this process involves a deep interchange of energy between two people, we also become more integrated and develop more fully as human beings. Through the consistent use of Therapeutic Touch, we, the "healers," are also healed. In fact, Krieger (1979) actually calls this technique a yoga of healing.

> It is because the interaction between healer and healee can become so highly personalized that I call it a yoga of healing. Through it, one learns to develop many latent human abilities; as in yoga, the expert practice of Therapeutic Touch demands concentration and a deep sense of commitment to lifting a little the veil of suffering of living beings. It is an effort so constant that it can become a way of life. (p. 71)

In this chapter, I will discuss some basic aspects of the theory and practice of Therapeutic Touch, focusing on its use in daily life. As a natural potential of human beings, the process of Therapeutic Touch is "twice blessed"; it enriches the lives of both giver and receiver.

Some Basic Principles of Therapeutic Touch

We commonly define Therapeutic Touch as touch with the conscious intent to heal (Krieger, 1973). Healing, in these terms, means assisting the individual to reorganize his/her energies so that he/she is again in dynamic balance. When using Therapeutic Touch, we have found it important to remember that it is the healee who ultimately has to heal him/herself. In acting the role of healer, we help the process along.

In discussing the principles of Therapeutic Touch, we may conceptualize the human being as an orderly, or potentially orderly, system of various energies. This is a different perspective from that of our traditional Western view of the human being as a solid, three-dimensional entity, distinctly separate from the environment. Our traditional understanding of the human body as composed of various tissues, which are composed of molecules, which, in turn, are composed of atoms, illustrates this Western view.

Although the idea of a human being as a system of energies is more consonant with Eastern than with Western culture, it is not totally incompatible with modern Western science. Physicists are now realizing more fully that atoms are not "things" like billiard balls; they are patterns of energy (Capra, 1975). Since atoms are considered the basic building blocks of the material world, it is possible to conceptualize a human being as a tremendously complex, dynamic pattern—i.e., field—of energy. An energy field, by its very nature, is a continuum; all aspects are interconnected. If we conceptualize a human being as an energy field, it follows that all aspects of his or her humanness—mind, emotions, physical processes—are interconnected in a dynamic manner.

Furthermore, the human being, as an energy field, is an open system with no rigid boundaries between self and the environment. Energies extend outward and can be directed from one person to another. Heat energy is an example of this process. We have all, at one time or another, held someone's cold hands in ours to warm them up through conduction. Emotional energy is another example. Often we can go into a room and "feel" someone's fear or love or hostility even though no words have been spoken and the person's back is toward us.

Many cultures, especially those of the East, recognize and have documented other subtle types of energy. An example is the Hindu concept of *prana*, the life force (Govinda, 1969). Krieger (1975) postulates that this is one of the healing energies operative in Therapeutic Touch.

Within the framework of Therapeutic Touch, health is that state in which all of an individual's energies are in harmony, or dynamic balance. Disease is a state of disequilibrium, blockage, and/or deficit in the flow of energy. Working with Therapeutic Touch, we first sensitize ourselves to the energy field of the healee and assess its condition. Then we knowledgeably and consciously help the person to repattern his/her energies in a healthier way.

The assessment process is very important. Even if someone tells me that the problem is a "chest cold," I still check the condition of his/her entire energy field. Since Therapeutic Touch is a holistic approach to care, I discern what role the cold plays in the general scheme of life events for this person. It is not the cold that

I am going to treat but the individual who has this cold, so I must gain knowledge about the quality of all his/her energies.

I do this by first centering myself—putting myself in a calm, alert, open state—and then attuning to the healee. I "listen," as it were, to the melody of his energies, and I use my hands to pick up any localized areas of congestion, dysrhythmia, or deficit.

In general, practitioners of Therapeutic Touch work with their hands in the finer aspect of the individual's energy field, about four to six inches beyond the surface of the physical body. Although one can administer Therapeutic Touch using actual body contact, the field beyond the surface of the body is less compacted so that dysrhythmias are more easily perceptible and the healing process proceeds more quickly. A casual observer might think that we are dealing with nothing more than thin air. However, if this observer would take some time to practice, he or she would soon become sensitive to these finer energies surrounding the body.

For the person with the chest cold, for example, I might pick up a sensation of heat or thickness over the chest area. To me, these sensations generally indicate a congestion of energy. Another practitioner, however, might have sensed this same congestion as tingling or pressure. Since our own, unique energy fields are our tools, we must learn how they operate. We have to become deeply aware of our own styles, discerning individually how we feel the various dysrhythmias such as congestion, pain, and anxiety. This is done through much practice and supervision. I have also found it helpful to keep a record of my experiences, for this gives isolated events a meaningful context for evaluation and understanding.

Very often my assessment of the energy field will differ from the medical diagnosis and/or from the patient's signs and symptoms. For example, a teenage girl told me that she had had a sore throat and low-grade fever for 15 days despite a course of antibiotics. On assessment, her throat felt fairly clear. However, the area around her kidneys was thick and heavy, which indicated to me that this area was congested. I helped to clear her field by using my hands to direct the "thickness" from the kidney area out through her feet. Then, as a traditional nurse would do, I sent her home with instructions to rest and take fluids. Interestingly enough, the very next day she called to say that the sore throat had disappeared.

The Use of Therapeutic Touch
on People with Colds

When many of my friends come down with a cold, they ask me for a "treatment." They feel that Therapeutic Touch relieves their congestion and speeds up the healing processes within them. Although no formal research has been done to confirm this as yet, practitioners will generally agree that individuals with the common cold respond very well to Therapeutic Touch. However, certain precautions must always be observed.

For example, suppose I am working with a person with a chest cold. With my hands, I can detect exactly where the congestion has localized in the field. As I stated above, I personally sense this as an area of "thickness" which can actually be removed from the field with a stroking motion. If I move the congestion away from the chest area but fail to take it completely out of the field, preferably through the feet, it can become established somewhere else and cause discomfort. It could end up in the stomach area creating nausea or in the bladder area creating spasm. Many elderly people have a sluggish flow of energy in their legs so I find that additional care must be taken to relieve this area. The energy field, therefore, is an open system that transcends definite organ systems and must be treated in a holistic manner.

Individuals suffering from colds generally have a deficit of energy. I sense this as a "pulling" sensation in various areas of their fields. When energy is transferred to these people, the disease process very often appears to "quicken."

For example, a short time ago I treated a young man whose chief complaint was a sore throat and low-grade fever. After an input of energy, his fever rose. In an hour or so his sore throat cleared and his chest became loose and congested. It was as though the disease process had to travel a certain course and it was now "trotting" instead of "walking."

I have learned that although this is a beneficial result, much care must be taken, especially when working with young children and people who are debilitated. Using the above analogy, I do not want the disease process to "gallop." Too much manipulation or an overload of energy can create discomfort and frighten the patient.

The very old, the very young, and the very ill are especially sensitive to the transfer of energy and thus a great deal of gentleness is required of the practitioner.

Many beginning practitioners find it difficult to tone down their energies so that they do not overwhelm the patient. Self-discipline, or self-modulation, however difficult, is one of the most important aspects of this type of healing. For if I cannot control my own energies, how can I possibly use them as a tool to help another person?

The Importance of Centering

Self-discipline, for practitioners of Therapeutic Touch, usually begins with the practice of centering. This is the act of focusing myself in the here-and-now, of placing myself in a calm, alert, open state of being. In general, when I lose my sense of inner calm, when I get anxious or irritated, I narrow my perceptual field. I do not pick up as much information from the world around me, and what information I do pick up is likely to become distorted. During the healing process, this is a huge drawback, because it makes me much less sensitive to the patient.

Also, if I am anxious or irritated, there is a good chance that the patient will be affected by my state of being. He, too, might very well become anxious or irritated, or just have a vague feeling that something is wrong. He might then withdraw from me, making the treatment more difficult, if not impossible, to accomplish.

This is understandable when we assume that human beings are energy fields with no rigid boundaries. We live in a state of constant energy interchange. When we practice Therapeutic Touch, we make use of this principle in a highly conscious and knowledgeable way.

Thus, if my friend has a headache and is very anxious about an exam, I can fill my being with a sense of peace and project this quality to him. As there is no distinct division between emotions and physiological processes in our paradigm, my friend's heartbeat might slow down, his muscle tension might decrease, and his headache might go away or at least become bearable.

Just as the patient will respond to the practitioner's state of being, so also does the practitioner respond to the state of the patient's energies. When I use Therapeutic Touch, my own energy field, as my tool, functions as an antenna, detecting the quality of the patient's field. If I am not focused, or integrated, these energies can overwhelm me; and instead of me helping to repattern the patient's field, he repatterns mine. In the above example, instead of being able to project a sense of peace to my friend, I would get caught up in his end-of-the-semester anxiety.

Maintaining a calm state is thus crucial for the healing process. But, as I said before, it can be extremely difficult. Fortunately, there are many techniques of centering and meditation available for us. A detailed description of these would be far beyond the scope of this chapter. However, as Claudio Naranjo has written (Naranjo and Ornstein, 1971), they all involve a "dwelling upon" something.

> While in most of one's daily life the mind flits from one subject or thought to another, and the body moves from one position to another, meditation practices generally involve an effort to stop this merry-go-round of mental or other activity and to set our attention upon a single object, sensation, utterance, issue, mental state, or activity. (p. 10)

One centering technique that I personally have found very helpful for healing is derived from a Buddhist meditation. The object dwelt upon is the emotion of love. To do this, I sit comfortably with my feet on the floor. I close my eyes and think of someone, or something, that I love very much. For a few minutes I just experience this feeling of love. This is important because in order to use this emotion in the healing process I must know exactly how it feels to me. When I have fully experienced the feeling of love within myself, I slowly let it radiate from me in all directions. I do not ever try to force it out; I just try to be very open and still, letting love flow through me as an open system.

This exercise, then, is one which has helped me to focus my energies more deeply. Through daily practice, it has helped me to recognize the quality of the energy of love and to direct it outward consciously to those who need it.

The Use of Therapeutic Touch
on People with Minor Wounds

Minor wounds are a common problem in day-to-day life. It is very tempting, when treating individuals with wounds, to focus all our attention on the cut and ignore the rest of the individual. This is especially true if the cut is painful and bleeding. However, this approach defeats our purpose: a partial or fragmented treatment gives very little help to the patient. Therapeutic Touch treats the individual holistically.

For example, a short time ago a friend of mine, while preparing dinner, slashed her index finger with a paring knife. As any well-educated nurse would do, I went into the bathroom for a bandage. Even after learning Therapeutic Touch, I still find the three-dimensional, solid view of reality very applicable for health care. However, when I shift my perspective and think in terms of energy fields, new avenues of nursing intervention are open to me.

After putting on the bandage, I centered myself quickly and assessed my friend's entire energy field. I picked up a "pulling" sensation in the kidney-adrenal area and around the cut finger. As I stated before, this sensation indicates to me that there is a deficit of energy. Permeating her field was a sensation of fine heaviness, which differs from the thicker heaviness of congestion. This suggested, along with the adrenal deficit, that my friend was in a fatigued state due to stress. As you can see, the assessment process combines the use of intuition, analysis, and acquired knowledge.

Acting as an open system in a universe of open systems, I channeled energy through myself to my friend—in particular, to those areas in which I sensed a deficit. I kept this up until the "pulling sensation" subsided. This, in effect, was her way of telling me that she had received all the energy she could assimilate at that time. If I had not been open to her feedback, I would have overloaded her.

I also extended to my friend a very gentle feeling of joy to help lighten the heavy condition of her field. Emotions have a great deal of leverage, so to speak. When I learned to use the emotional aspect of my field consciously, in a therapeutic manner, I found that the healing process proceeded more quickly and that it had a deeper and more lasting effect. Therefore, by shifting my perspective, I was able to see that the cut finger was only one aspect of a much larger pattern. In this view, treating only the finger would have been grossly inadequate.

Therapeutic Touch: An Act of Cultivation

As practitioners of Therapeutic Touch, we follow all the basic principles; we learn to center ourselves and modulate our energies, to assess with sensitivity and to treat holistically. In the end, however, patients heal themselves. In spite of our expectations, they always get better in their own way. Some inner principle sifts the energy, so to speak, and integrates it according to its own needs.

For example, a few months ago I treated a woman who had a bad headache. After I completed the treatment she told me: "You know I still have this headache. But something is happening to me...you know the problem I told you about with Joe...Well, I think I see it from another angle now."

I did not give her the insight about her family problem. It came entirely from within her own being. The observable problem, the headache, remained but something deeper, more important to the individual, had been touched. I had acted only as a facilitator.

There appears to be in all living things an inner drive toward wholeness, which Therapeutic Touch is able to bolster. Progoff (1963) writes:

> The essence of the psyche is that it is the directive principle by means of which meaning unfolds in the individual's existence. It is a principle that operates not only in human beings but in sub-human specise as well. The tendency is observed throughout the natural world that individual beings are drawn in a direction that fulfills the potentialities of their nature. The psyche is the faculty by means of which this occurs. When the principle of meaning, which the psyche embodies, is experienced intensely by an individual, it has the effect of opening in him a sensitivity to meaningfulness not only in his personal life but in the universe around him (p. 80).

Thus, I feel that Therapeutic Touch is a process of helping an individual to realign himself or herself with this inner directive principle so that it can manifest again in daily life. For both healer and healee, it is an act of cultivation, in which the inner "seed" or growth potential is nourished.

Bibliography

Capra, F. *The tao of physics.* Berkeley: Shambhala Publications, 1975.

Govinda, L. A. *Foundations of Tibetan mysticism.* New York: Samuel Weiser, 1969.

Krieger, D. (Ed.) *The Therapeutic Touch: how to use your hands to help or to heal.* Englewood Cliffs, N.J.: Prentice-Hall, 1979.

Krieger, D. Therapeutic Touch: the imprimatur of nursing, *American Journal of Nursing,* 1975, 75, 784–786.

Krieger, D. The relationship of touch, with intent to help or heal, to subjects' in-vivo hemoglobin values: a study in personalized interaction. In *Proceedings of the ninth ANA nursing research conference.* Kansas City: American Nurses' Association, 1973.

Naranjo, C. and Ornstein, R. *On the psychology of meditation.* New York: Viking Press, 1971.

Progoff, I. *The symbolic and the real.* New York: McGraw-Hill Book Company, 1963.

Chapter 5

Therapeutic Touch: One Nurse's Evolution as a Healer

Janet Quinn

Five years ago I was graduated from a four-year baccalaureate program. Armed with 60 (count 'em—60) credits of nursing to ensure my professional competence, and 68 credits of arts, science, and humanities to "round me out," I emerged with the confidence of a veteran matador about to begin his umpteenth bullfight.

I had worked my way through school doing general medical and surgical nursing, so I decided to tackle bigger and better things. My sword raised high, I marched headlong into the arena to do battle with the bulls of illness and pain, death and dying.

I worked first in an emergency room. "*This* is nursing," I said. Then I moved to the medical ICU, "Now this *is* nursing," I thought, as I became more and more proficient in the care and maintenance of complex machinery, with people attached. "Now this is *professional* nursing," I thought, as I diagnosed arrhythmias and "suggested" to the new interns what medication we should use to treat that arrhythmia, somehow *also* with a person attached. Yes, I was winning the battle.

With this belief in mind, it was a mystery to me why I faithfully read the help-wanted classified ads, always looking—but for what? For the teaching position that I found one lucky day, and secured the next.

Reproduced, with permission, from Janet Quinn, "One Nurse's Evolution as a Healer." *American Journal of Nursing*, April. Vol. 79 No. 4. Copyright ©1979, American Journal of Nursing Company.

By the end of that first year of teaching, I was hard pressed even to define professional nursing. I enjoyed my students and loved seeing them grow. I taught them the importance of nursing the whole person. I demonstrated techniques for helping patients talk about their fears and anxieties. But somehow, in the clinical area, I got as tied up as ever in the mechanics of irrigating the NG tube, care of the colostomy, regulating the IV, and so on and so on.

A discontent began growing, and a small voice inside kept asking, "Is this all there is?" I was, after all, a professional nurse, a teacher at that. And I loved nursing, didn't I? I resigned at the end of the year. It occurred to me that somewhere I had lost my sword; the bulls were winning.

When all else fails, I had heard, you go to graduate school. This I did. Beginning the master's progam at New York University was something akin to entering the Twilight Zone. Instead of the belief system that, "What you see is what you get," I was suddenly inundated with concepts like "Man is an energy field, the physical body being only *part* of what you get," and "Illness is an imbalance in the energy flow of the system."

In those early days with Martha Rogers, I often entertained the idea that the whole nursing department was a bit touched, and for the sake of my own sanity I should resign. However, I *was* learning, so I decided to stay. Besides, I didn't want to fool with the "unidirectionality of the universe"!

In February of 1976, I began a course with Dr. Dolores Krieger, who was beginning to teach about the "laying-on of hands" as a nursing modality. I was skeptical, but somehow I sensed that what was happening there was important. I stayed with it, sometimes in spite of my extreme anxiety, or maybe because of it. I learned that in the laying-on of hands, the self is used as an energy transmitter. But one thought plagued me. If the transmitter is blocked or faulty, the energy given out will be full of static. For the first time, I was forced to examine the *self*, who was the *nurse*. It wasn't enough anymore to assume that I loved people, that my motivation was pure and altruistic, that I was a very sensitive person. I had to know.

The process of exploring one's depths is exhilarating. It is also painful and tedious work. But, as anyone who has taken the trip knows, you can't turn back once you've started.

I was, for a time, paralyzed by self-doubts in terms of Therapeutic Touch. I could not feel the cues that Dr. Krieger and my classmates discussed, and when I attempted to send energy, I felt only anxiety. I believed in Therapeutic Touch as a human potential, but felt myself unable, or perhaps unwilling, to make a commitment.

The following summer, I went to Pumpkin Hollow Farm in New York, to attend a two-week workshop on Therapeutic Touch. Those first days were among the most traumatic in my life. I was bombarded by stimuli. Surrounded by healers who were healing, my paralyzed ego was afraid and threatened. "I'm a failure." "I can't do it." "They're better than me." I hurt. But I was in the right place with my pain.

Since we interact with our total environment, it is difficult to say whether the positive force at the workshop was the people or the magnificent country—with its rushing river and towering spruce trees. It matters not; something was happening.

One day I was working with a client with a more experienced member of the group, and suddenly I felt *connected*. I started picking up the elusive cues from the client in our assessment, and my partner validated them. My hands somehow seemed to know what needed to be done, and I let them lead me. I felt the energy of the client balance and even out, and again my partner validated. My interaction had finally been therapeutic and beneficial. It was a miraculous day, which I shall never forget.

When one discovers a bit of the truth, it always seems so obvious. What I learned that day was how to stop thinking about me. I had been so caught up in worrying about *myself*—was *I* sensitive enough, could *I* do it—that, of course, it was impossible to make contact with anyone else. When, somehow, I surrendered my ego, for better or for worse, I realized what healing is really all about.

It's been almost two years since that workshop. I have been using Therapeutic Touch with friends, family, colleagues, and patients. I have outgrown my fascination with machines and have almost stopped worrying about my personal success or failure as a healer.

Many of us who have become involved with such an alternative modality have firsthand knowledge about the effects of Therapeutic Touch on the client. We have seen the relaxation when a client's pain leaves him. We have watched a restless patient become calm and a withdrawn patient respond—"evidence," if you will, that changes are taking place in the client.

We also know that at the time that we are involved with that client, we are in some ways no longer separate from him, that we are part of the same open energy system. The nature of open systems is such that a change in the part leads to a change in the whole. The obvious conclusion, then, is that if the client is changed by the interaction, then the nurse must also be changed. What is the nature of that change? Can it be measured? Predicted? Controlled? I will share with you some of my experiential answers.

I know for certain that using Therapeutic Touch has changed and continues to change me. Including alternative modalities of healing in one's practice requires a certain philosophy, and this change or expansion of philosophy pervades one's total existence. My views of the universe, of the people in it, and of myself have all changed. My concepts of illness and health have so altered that I can no longer nurse anyone without trying to understand why that person needs to be sick *now*. What are the "dispiriting events" (Jourard, 1971, p. 76) in this client's life that are being manifested through illness?

I have evolved a philosophy of professional nursing that guides my practice and leaves me fulfilled instead of frustrated. Nursing is, after all, "a special case of loving" (Jourard, 1971, p. 207).

Now, what of the changes in the nurse during a therapeutic interchange? Again, I will answer for myself. It seems that the nature of the change is indeed a manifestation of the principle of synchrony, which states: "Change in the human field depends only upon the state of the human field and the simultaneous state of the environmental field at any given point in space-time" (Rogers, 1970).

If, during the interaction, I am able to be completely centered and open to the universal energy around me, then I am left feeling quiet, peaceful, and energized. These are the times (and it is no coincidence) when, I believe, the patient has received the optimum benefit as well.

On the other hand, if I am, for some reason, not really open to the environment, much of the energy I am giving is my own. I am then left feeling tired, a bit sad, and ineffectual. This is a phenomenon that has been discussed by Dr. Krieger, as well as other nurses with whom I have spoken. It seems important, then, for the healer to be certain that he or she is acting as the *transmitter* of energy, and not the generator. This is a skill that I am still trying to perfect, and unfortunately, I still sometimes don't know which I am being until I feel the aftereffects.

I believe, then, that the nature of the change is such that the healer's energy pattern and its distribution are altered simultaneously with the changes occurring in the client's energy pattern. The direction of that change can be predicted and controlled, but only through the disciplined consciousness of the healer. Although the change can be felt subjectively after the interaction, we will have to develop indices sensitive enough to make the measurement of energy patterns objective.

In my evolution as a nurse healer, I went from idealistic new graduate, through disenchantment, and somehow ended up as an idealistic, *older* graduate. In many ways, I have come full circle. I am happy to say that I am back in the arena again, and although I still have much to learn, I have found my sword. That sword is Therapeutic Touch.

Bibliography

Jourard, S. M. *The transparent self*. 2nd ed. New York: D. Van Nostrand Co., 1971.

Rogers, M. *An introduction to the theoretical basis of nursing*. Philadelphia: F. A. Davis Co., 1970, p. 98.

Chapter 6

Therapeutic Touch for Children and Their Families

Diana Finnerin

The purposes of this chapter are to present the various uses and some effects of Therapeutic Touch upon children and their families in a pediatric hospital setting and to provide some findings that will stimulate further research to expand the theoretical base for Therapeutic Touch. The uses of Therapeutic Touch for children and their families are as numerous as the children and families who are treated. However, I have selected three specific case studies for presentation. Each case study is representative of numerous similar cases in which Therapeutic Touch was found to be useful in reducing clinical symptoms of fever, intestinal inflammation, and purpura and in assisting with bone healing.

Case Study: Baby Jim

Baby Jim was a six-month-old child admitted with a diagnosis of gastroenteritis, an acute inflammation of the stomach and intestine. He had had frequent vomiting and diarrhea for the previous three days and was bordering on severe dehydration. He had no tears, his skin turgor was poor, and he was lethargic and highly irritable when touched. His electrolytes were imbalanced, and his temperature was 103.4°F.

Following the initial admitting procedures, an intravenous infusion was begun to replace fluids and reestablish electrolyte balance, thus rehydrating Baby Jim. His parents, who were quite upset by this invasive proceeding, left for a brief period in the hope that their baby would fall off to sleep. Instead, he continued to whimper weakly, unable to sleep with all extremities restrained and in strange surroundings. He most probably was experiencing acute gastrointestinal symptoms.

At this time, I performed Therapeutic Touch on Baby Jim for a short time. Twenty minutes later, he was asleep and his temperature was 99.4°F without an antipyretic agent or a cooling sponge bath. He slept for approximately three hours and forty-five minutes. While Jim was sleeping his parents returned and I found them still quite anxious. They were surprised to see their baby sleeping. I explained to them that I had been able to calm him and help him to fall asleep by a process that let him sense an inner quietness and peace within me. That state of calm was "transferred' to him, and this process was known as Therapeutic Touch. I asked them if they would like to experience Therapeutic Touch in order to better understand what was helping, and they consented.

I led Baby Jim's parents through a brief relaxation meditation in which they allowed themselves to become as completely relaxed as possible. I asked them to imagine that a gentle blue light was filling the room. I placed my hands on Mrs. J's solar plexus (the area above the waist) and together we imagined the blue light gently filtering into her solar plexus. She became noticeably calmer and began to cry. I sensed her tensions and fears of illness and the negative feelings she had of past hospital experiences. I remained with her, supporting her and sending "energies" to her during the entire time.

While Mrs. J cried, her husband approached her. I moved back and placed my hand on him, providing Therapeutic Touch for him, as he supported his wife with love and care. Both began to cry in each other's arms with open communication. Near the end, both Mr. and Mrs. J expressed the belief that they did not understand what had just transpired, but felt it to be a beautiful experience. They now felt more in control and had more strength and confidence in their own ability to handle the crisis. We hugged and thanked each other.

After I left the room, I felt warm and beautiful inside. I felt good about myself and thankful again that I had learned to use Therapeutic Touch in what seemed like a "helpless" situation.

When Baby Jim awoke he was actually cheerful and more alert.

In eight hours his electrolytes were within normal limits. His intravenous infiltrated during the night and it was discontinued. He was placed on oral fluids, and he had no further stools or emesis for 18 hours. On the following morning Baby Jim was discharged with a progressively normal diet. Not all applications of Therapeutic Touch in babies with gastroenteritis are as dramatic as Baby Jim's. However, we have observed that recovery periods are shorter and without complications in babies and children receiving Therapeutic Touch.

Case Study: Howie

Howie was a 13-year-old boy who had sustained a fracture of his femur in an auto accident. Due to the extent of the fracture, it was anticipated that sufficient calcification or healing would occur in approximately six to eight weeks' time so that a cast could then be applied. Howie's femur was pinned and he was placed in skeletal traction the day of admission. His pain was intense.

His nurse, Jane, and I were with him at that time. Jane explained that she could feel heat right over the area of his fracture. Howie reached over and said he noticed the difference in temperature as he passed his hand over his fracture. Jane further explained that she had learned a technique in which she could move the heat away with her hands and as the heated area became balanced (i.e., cooler), the pain would subside. Howie asked Jane to try anything she knew to relieve him of his increasing discomfort. Jane looked to Howie's parents. They too nodded consent. Jane began Therapeutic Touch on Howie by first centering, i.e., finding the quietest place within her own self. She placed her hands, one on each side of the fractured painful area. She imaged a balanced, cooling energy passing through her right hand into the fracture site. She experienced the flow as a cool, calm, resonating energy at times. Jane would shake off the heat which was accumulating on her left hand as if it were droplets of water. She imaged Howie as the happy, whole, running athlete he normally was. Within ten minutes, Howie fell off to sleep without medication. Three hours later he awoke less tense and with only mild discomfort.

Howie told everyone of his "weird" experience with Therapeutic Touch and how it really worked. His parents, who were present during the entire session, asked many questions and along with Howie asked that Therapeutic Touch be done whenever needed. He received Therapeutic Touch every day from Jane and his leg healed well enough in three weeks' time to be casted. The physicians on the case refused to believe the x-ray reports and they ordered a second x-ray after seeing the first one. They could find no logical explanation for the rapid healing process. Mystified, they kept Howie in traction for three additional weeks. An attempt was made to present the concepts of Therapeutic Touch to the physicians by the nurse, by Howie's parents, and by myself, but this was dismissed as "nonreality."

In our experience, it seems that teenagers respond with much openness to discussions about Therapeutic Touch. Our personal records indicate that teenagers who have spent from two to three months in the hospital, regularly receiving Therapeutic Touch, seem to have an increased ability to communicate with their families and the hospital personnel. Comments are frequently heard, such as, "I can't believe this is my son; he's so warm and friendly. We're actually talking with one another." Heightened creativity is also demonstrated by beautiful art work, poetry, and the playing of musical instruments. We notice that those teens not receiving Therapeutic Touch appear more withdrawn, exhibiting greater hostility and anger throughout their hospital stay. They become TV addicts and refuse attempts of the recreational therapists to channel their energies into constructive activities.

Case Study: Jamie

Jamie was an eight-year-old boy admitted with abdominal pain and skin rash. He was diagnosed as possibly having Henoch-Schoenlein's disease. Because of his poor response to medication and the worsening of his abdominal pain, he was taken to surgery with the expectation of a possible abscess, internal bleeding, or other clinical complication. Jamie's intestines were grossly inflamed and his original diagnosis was confirmed. He was returned to his preoperative medical regimen. Jamie continued to show no improvement. For the first time in two postoperative days, while Jamie was expressing severe physical discomfort, I asked him if I could do something to help him feel more comfortable. I told him I would not have to touch him, especially since he was so uncomfortable. I told him that I would hold my hands over his "tummy" and imagine that he was all better and that he was outside playing with his friends. Jamie smiled and said OK. He watched cautiously at first. Soon his appearance changed from tension and doubt to relaxation and trust. He became noticeably calmer, his respirations were slower and deeper, and he quietly fell off to sleep. Later that evening he continued to complain of abdominal pain. He was carefully observed throughout the evening and morning hours. In the early morning I performed Therapeutic Touch on Jamie for a second time. The field of energy around his abdomen felt different than on the preceding day. I sensed his problem localizing and subsiding. Upon being questioned, Jamie said that the pain was "only in one place, and not all over like it was before." I alerted the physicians of this change. They examined Jamie and he was again taken to surgery to rule out a possible complication. To the surgeon's surprise, Jamie's intestines were clear and shining. He exhibited virtually a completely healed bowel.

Clinically, Jamie presented a bewildering picture. The physicians were mystified and could not explain the negative findings, particularly when three days earlier his intestinal picture had been so glaringly poor. Fortunately, this physician was familiar with Therapeutic Touch. He listened as I explained that I had performed Therapeutic Touch on Jamie twice. In light of our conversation and subsequent discussion with Jamie's parents, the doctor decided to "sit on the case" and use Therapeutic Touch as an adjunct therapy. Within two days Jamie's symptoms began to subside and gradually they disappeared. The entire staff was astounded by the disappearance of symptoms and it was agreed that some unexplained factor was at work and needed further investigation.

Use of Imagery and Therapeutic Touch with Children and Their Families

Imagery, or visualization, may be used during healing by Therapeutic Touch or as an adjunct to Therapeutic Touch. It is man's vision of himself as whole and unified with his environment which is so critical to states of health or illness. On our pediatric unit we like to instruct parents to use visualization techniques, because we believe that with children the family circle contributes to the health–illness process. The family's psychosocial patterns, such as alliances, scapegoating, and labeling, as well as the parents' perceptions of their ill child, play an important role in the process of getting well. The pediatric unit provides a fertile field for therapeutic intervention in which healing is expedited by the nurse who works "with and through" the family to enhance the child's return to health. The use of imagery by parents or family members tends to replace those habitual processes such as excessive worry, blame, and guilt, which feed the development and growth of illness in a family.

In the clinical example of Jamie, his mother sat in constant attendance at his bedside. She frequently sought out the nursing staff to ask for something she could do to help her son. Her feelings of powerlessness, fear, and anxiety concerning Jamie's future were paramount in her life at that time. Aside from the few physical ministrations she could perform, it was suggested that perhaps she would like to use a "powerful" healing tool while she sat at Jamie's bedside for long hours. She readily consented. A number of meaningful imagery concepts were worked out with her.

She was often hypnotized by the intravenous drops as they bounced out of the IV solution into the dropper through the tubing, and into Jamie's body. Therefore, in her visualization process, she began to image the antibiotic as a powerful phagocyte that destroyed all the infectious organisms contributing to Jamie's problems. Thus, rather than sitting at her son's bedside in fear and worry she repatterned and activated her thought processes to provide a positive milieu of health for Jamie.

Together, Jamie and his mother planned an imagery trip to relieve his pain. They began their imaging as soon as Jamie began to experience an episode of discomfort. Initially they would relax as instructed, then visualize the pain passing into a bubble and slowly blowing off into the distance. Even after discharge the patterns of communication between Jamie and his mother continued. Her growth toward the use of positive thought patterns in her daily life experiences was quite remarkable. This was possibly the most health-producing intervention the hospital staff offered this family.

Imagery in conjunction with Therapeutic Touch has also proven infinitely valuable in working with the dying child. Anna, a 12-year-old child, was in the terminal stages of a fatal blood dyscrasia. Her brother had died of the same disease one year before. Her fear of death and its meaning to her were uppermost in her thoughts, yet Anna chose never to speak openly of her plight. Rather, she spoke through the use of symbols. The staff began to work with Anna using imagery.

During episodes of extreme discomfort, Anna's nurse took her on an imagery trip. Leaving her pain-filled body, Anna would romp through a field of flowers with her pet goat, smelling the flowers and feeling the breeze blow gently on her face. While Anna was experiencing her imagery trip, Therapeutic Touch was administered by myself, Jane, or the evening RN.

Moments before Anna's death, she called for her nurse to take her on her imagery trip to her favorite place. During this last trip Anna was able to separate peacefully from the world and die without fear.

The use of Therapeutic Touch allied with the use of imagery techniques for children and their family members has proven an indispensable tool on the pediatric unit. It has served as a mechanism through which channels of communication are established and healing love is readily imparted.

Frequently when positive family bonding is evident the parents themselves may be used to administer Therapeutic Touch. This may be the method of choice when the child is anxious and fearful of the nurse, or when he is at an age in which he responds more naturally to his parents. At times such as these it is recognized that the flow of energy between the body field of parent and child are in such harmony that Therapeutic Touch is then readily imparted directly by or through the parent with little instruction required. This technique of working through the parent is accomplished by placing one's hands on the parent and channeling healing energy through him/her to the child. Usually the child and parent become visibly relaxed and often the child falls off to sleep.

Not every nurse on our pediatric unit utilizes Therapeutic Touch in her daily nursing practices, yet each in her own way has incorporated various facets of the Therapeutic Touch process into her professional and personal activities. For example, one nurse uses centering as a means for calming herself with a distressed, screaming infant, another teaches imagery to parents and children to enhance self-healing, and yet another has the uncanny ability to create calm during a heightened crisis situation.

Most staff members who do not utilize Therapeutic Touch will still readily seek out those of us who do, and all the staff have come to know what a nurse means when she asks Jane or me to go into a room and "please do your thing."

As I have tried to relate in this chapter, Therapeutic Touch can have a profound effect upon any and all who use it. In our Pediatric Department it has become a catalyst for growth, creativity, and love. It has produced a state of being that we define as a state of love, affecting not only our professional roles but every facet of our existence.

Chapter 7

The Use of Therapeutic Touch in the Nursing Care of the Terminally Ill Person

Mary E. Mueller Jackson

Theoretical Foundations

One of the most challenging directions in nursing today is the care of the person through terminal illness. Recent interest in the dying process and in death is evidenced by the quantity of literature available in both nursing and non-nursing publications (Kutscher, 1974). Concurrent with the proliferation of thanatology literature have been the publications and research concerning alternative modalities of healing including acupuncture, spiritual healing, nutritional approaches, and Therapeutic Touch (Ingrasci, 1978).

Several trends in health care which are relevant to this discussion of Therapeutic Touch with the terminally ill person become apparent from this body of literature. First, dying and death have made a transition from the family–church system in the direction of the professional–hospital system (Aries, 1974). The process of dying occurs primarily in the hospital, often without the presence of the family and extended support systems. Second, the health care consumer is exploring adjuncts to and alternatives for the medical model of health care delivery due to the limitations of conventional systems of health care (Weinstein, 1978). A discussion of this trend in depth is outside the limitations of this chapter, but it is important to illustrate this movement as it does influence the individual's choice of treatment modalities. The third trend is philosophical in nature and concerns the definition of health. The concept of health is being redefined in ways other than the pathological one which equates health with the absence of disease (Reilly, 1975). According to Krieger (1979), health is considered to be a harmonious relationship between the individual and his total environment. There is postulated a continual interacting flow of energy from the environment to the various levels of the individual. Within this context, disease is a disturbance in the free flow of *prana* (Krieger, 1975). Rogers (1970) discusses "maximum health potential" in this man–environment interaction and states that one's health is redefined continually as the life process evolves "irreversibly and unidirectionally" (p. 59). There is also emerging an alteration in health care concepts for a "new age" which holds the individual responsible for his/her own health or illness (Roggenbuck, 1978).

The implications of these trends for professional practice are significant. They are exemplified, for instance, by the Patient's Bill of Rights and the development of patient's ombudsman positions. The individual is becoming recognized as a unique being, taking responsibility for many aspects of his/her health care. The subjective experience of wellness is influenced by but not subjected to one's environment.

Health and wellness are no longer seen as exclusively physical in their parameters. The capability for growth and development as a whole person, even in the face of life-threatening illness, is an emergent criterion in assessing levels of wellness. The normal responses to impending death and the accompanying developmental stages of anticipatory grief are often blocked and interrupted by chronic pain, the stressful anxiety of hospitalization, treatment, and the interruption of one's life work (Lindeman, 1965). These secondary manifestations often become the primary standard by which the individual's state of health or ill-health is assessed. The intensification of the pain–anxiety spiral often leads to hopelessness and despair in the end stages of the disease process. Many individuals are also prevented from participating fully in the process of dying by the "unfinished business" of their lives (Kübler-Ross, 1969). It is my belief that Therapeutic Touch is a treatment modality that can relieve pain and reduce anxiety so that this capacity for growth and development is not impeded in the final stages of life.

Therapeutic Touch: An Intervention for the Dying Person

Therapeutic Touch has become an invaluable intervention for me to help relieve dying patients of the secondary complications mentioned above. The following study is an example of how I was able to assist one patient to complete her primary grieving and "finish the business" which was keeping her from a peaceful death.

Marilyn, a 54-year-old married woman, mother of one daughter and grandmother of two boys, was admitted to the hospital for blood transfusion in the treatment of leukemia. Despite the fatigue and weakness secondary to severe anemia and the threat of infection with a perilously low white cell count, she was ambulatory and independent in her activities of daily care. She was amicable and cooperative.

While on night duty in charge of the unit, I spent many hours with Marilyn, who had recently developed insomnia and was unable to sleep until nearly dawn. As her illness progressed, she was experiencing increasing pain and an intolerance for the multiple medications and transfusions she was receiving. After several days she began complaining of loss of appetite, restlessness, and shortness of breath.

One night shortly after one of her frequent doses of morphine, she called the nurses' station asking for more medication. Upon entering her room, I found her in bed tightly curled in the fetal position, eyes closed, grimacing and rigid with pain, complaining that she could not breathe. This episode was different from her usual wave pattern of pain. Recently I had noticed that Marilyn was becoming increasingly depressed, and I decided to spend a few more minutes assessing the situation before calling the doctor.

I asked her if I could put my hand on the place where it hurt and use a touch technique that sometimes works with pain such as hers. She agreed and I gently placed one hand on her back. I took her pulse with the other hand and timed her respirations; pulse was 96 per minute and respirations were 58 per minute. I then began Therapeutic Touch. The assessment revealed to me an area of strong heat in the area of her pelvis and lower back and a tingling sensation radiating around her head. After several minutes she said the pain was "letting up a bit" and that she felt a wave of heat, "kind of like sunlight," from head to toe. Her respirations had decreased to 28 per minute and her body was slowly uncurling from the tight position. After ten minutes her pulse was 60 and her hands rested comfortably at her sides. She said she felt much better, and "lighter," then asked if I could stay and talk.

After I had been with her for a few minutes, she began to relate the thoughts leading up to her "attack." She told me how she had been wanting to talk to someone about her illness and that her husband, by recent marriage, had lost his first wife with cancer. She felt she was causing him additional suffering. They had been very close until recently; now she felt angry, bitter, and unable to talk to him about many "important things." She said she knew she didn't have much time and wanted to spend it with her husband and family. She was experiencing rapid changes in her body, and even though she was independent, she was afraid of the time when she would no longer be able to care for herself. "I'm a very vain woman, and I always want Frank to remember me the way he's used to seeing me." Marilyn had heard that very sick people often don't wear their dentures and "look messed up" in bed. She asked, "Do you know why I always wear blue nightgowns? Because Frank met me in an 'Alice-blue' gown and it reminds him of the early days before I got sick....I want to be sure that I will look nice. You know, have my teeth in, my hair combed, and be wearing a blue gown when I die. I can't tell Frank any of this, but you understand, don't you?" The next evening I saw Frank and asked his consent to use Therapeutic Touch if Marilyn wanted to continue.

Over the course of the next several nights, Marilyn did ask to continue Therapeutic Touch. She also asked if she could write down some of her wishes about funeral arrangements. She wanted to be buried in a nonsectarian plot so that she and Frank could eventually be together. To the list she added that she wanted her dentures put in at death "for Frank," and then requested that the list be entered as a part of her official chart.

The second week of hospitalization Marilyn had suffered drastic changes. Her red cell count had stabilized and the transfusions were discontinued after two days. Her white cell count had dropped so low that mask precautions were begun. This caused another barrier, a physical one, between herself and her husband.

Her use of morphine also stabilized. She comfortably tolerated longer intervals between doses, despite her rapid physical deterioration. She spent most of the day in bed, sleeping and reading Kübler-Ross' book *Questions and Answers on Death and Dying*, hiding it when her husband came to visit. Discussions during that time were concerned with losing her family. She cried more these days and wanted them to share what she had written the week before.

On days off, I would visit Marilyn in the evening usually before Frank arrived from work. We would continue talking until the family came, we would all spend time together, and then I would leave. One night, however, we were talking about the list of wishes in the chart when Frank and Edris, her daughter, walked in. I asked Marilyn if she would like to continue talking. She agreed and as they listened, Frank began to cry. Marilyn told me she could finish the long-awaited conversation alone with her family. I left the room and waited. Frank finally came out and seeing me he said, "I had no idea. . . I have been so afraid of this for so long, but I am so glad we could share this together."

As a result of a reaction to a flu vaccine, I was to be out of work for two days and called Marilyn to tell her this. She anxiously expressed that she would miss me and the "touch" treatments. She hoped I felt better.

The third day I felt it was necessary to see Marilyn before the shift started and visited her in the evening. Upon entering her room, I found her alone, unresponsive, and manifesting similar patterns as the night that she had her severe "pain attack." Her pulse was over 100 and her respirations were shallow and nearly 60 per minute. She was dressed in a hospital gown and her dentures were in a container at the bedside. The physician's Continuation Notes revealed that Marilyn had gone into coma the night before, and that there was evidence now of a developing pneumonia. He had ordered private nurses. She was alone at the moment, as her family had gone out to the sitting room and her private nurse was busy in the nurse's station.

Re-entering the room, I identified myself and told Marilyn that I was feeling better and that I had come to give her a "touch" treatment. I told her that I knew she was too weak to respond and that all of her needs would be attended to. I talked about all the difficulties she had faced and how she had demonstrated so much courage and strength to talk to her family as she did. I told her I wanted to turn her onto her back, her favorite position, and begin the treatment. It was difficult to move her as she was quite tense and inflexible.

I began the treatment and within several minutes Marilyn's pulse and respirations had slowed to 56 and 16, respectively; her arms and legs were relaxed and movable. After several more minutes her vital functions had ceased. I stopped treatment, said my "good-byes" to Marilyn and began to change her into her blue gown. At that moment, her private duty nurse walked into the room and helped me with the gown. I asked her to stay until I brought her family in before she routinely notified the doctor.

As I accompanied Frank, Edris, and other family members into the room, Frank began to cry and noticed that we had forgotten to put Marilyn's dentures in place. He went to her table and placed them himself and smoothed her hair. I motioned for the nurse to leave the family alone so that they could spend the remaining few minutes with Marilyn to say "good-bye." Frank commented on how peaceful Marilyn looked since he had seen her only a half hour ago. Marilyn's wishes were being fulfilled exactly as she had wanted.

Discussion

In the above intervention, Marilyn's process of anticipatory grief and the completion of "unfinished business" were obstructed by her anxiety and depression, uncontrolled pain, and the stresses of hospitalization and separation from her traditional support systems. symptoms she had been experiencing early during her hospitalization were possibly side effects of medication. However, such symptoms have also been identified by Lindemann (1965) as part of the symptomatology of normal grief. So often these symptoms in the dying person are chemically treated and go unrecognized as manifestations of the grief process.

When I offered to "put my hand where it hurts," an underlying message was communicated to Marilyn. Krieger (1978) has referred to this interaction in the following way: "Touching tells the healee, 'I want to help'; allowing the touch by the healer says, 'Yes, I accept your help.' " For Marilyn, Therapeutic Touch was a useful adjunct to pain medication schedules. It produced a physiological relaxation and a decrease in anxiety which facilitated her movement through the grief process, and it helped her to "finish her business."

All patients do not respond to Therapeutic Touch as Marilyn did. It is not a panacea. However, those who are willing to "let go" of their attachment to their illness as a reason for their behavior and trust another in mutual support through the dying process will benefit from Therapeutic Touch. Each individual uses the interactional energy exchange in the way that is best suited to the fulfillment of his/her own goals and needs prior to death.

Krieger (1975) reports a rise in hemoglobin levels during Therapeutic Touch. I have found there is also a stabilization of hemoglobin level when it is used on a regular basis. This was an important adjunct for Marilyn because of the persistance of her hemolytic disease.

In caring for the unresponsive or comatose person with Therapeutic Touch, several factors need to be considered. In this state the energy exchange between the individual and the environment never reaches a threshold that would enable the individual to move through coma to a responsive state or transition to death. The result is a prolonged, unresponsive "plateau" existence. The healer, in practicing Therapeutic Touch, directs energy to the comatose person allowing him/her to utilize it for recovery or passage to death. The subtle changes in the energy field which are "sensed" in the hands during the assessment phase determine the length and duration of the treatments.

For me, using Therapeutic Touch in caring for persons through the terminal processes of life is both a rewarding and a difficult work. After all other treatments have been terminated, Therapeutic Touch remains as a vital intervention for nurse, patient, and family. It functions as a sign of hope, which in the final stages of life may mean the last lingering hope for recovery or hope for a comfortable, peaceful death.

Bibliography

Aries, P. *Western attitudes toward death*. Baltimore: Johns Hopkins University Press, 1974.

Ingrasci, R. Holistic health. *New Age*, 1978, 3, 47.

Krieger, D. Therapeutic Touch: the imprimatur of nursing. *American Journal of Nursing*, 1975, 75, 784–787.

Krieger, D. Postgraduate seminar, New York University, 1978.

Krieger, D. *The Therapeutic Touch: how to use your hands to help or to heal*. Englewood Cliffs, N.J.: Prentice-Hall, 1979.

Kübler-Ross, E. *Questions and answers on death and dying*. New York: Macmillan, 1969.

Kutscher, A.H. *A bibliography of books on death; bereavement, loss, and grief* (1935–1968; 1968–1972). New York: Health Sciences Publishing Company, 1974.

Lindemann, E. Symptomatology and management of acute grief, in Parad, H. (Ed.), *Crisis intervention: selected readings*. New York: Family Service Association of America, 1965.

Reilly, D. E. *Behavioral objectives in nursing*. New York: Appleton-Century-Crofts, 1975.

Rogers, M.E. *An introduction to the theoretical basis of nursing*. Philadephia: F.A. Davis, 1970.

Roggenbuck, P.E. The good news about cancer. *New Age*, 1978, 3, 32–35, 84–87.

Salzberg, C. The mystery of the healing hands. *Sunday News Magazine, New York Daily News*, February 25, 1979, 19–20.

Weinstein, N. The wary consumer's guide to alternative therapies. *New Age*, 1978, 3, 51–55.

Chapter 8

Therapeutic Touch in the Operating Room: Best of Both Worlds

Anne Marie H. Jonasen

The surgical suite is a place in which modern technology has excelled. Behind the operating doors, much has been done to save and enhance the lives of millions of people. Many patients come through this threshold daily, as the perimeters of providing surgical intervention continue to expand rapidly.

However, in this sterile environment, too often kindness and human contact are lost in favor of an aseptic isolation. It is the body or physical aspects of the patient that are the focus of concern by the surgeon and other team members. Often the "person" beneath the incision is lost. The mental, emotional, and spiritual aspects of the person are often neglected before and during surgical intervention. My intent during the time I have been an OR nurse has been to find that human being. It is from this perspective that I have utilized Therapeutic Touch, for I view it essentially as a humanistic approach to care. In this chapter I would like to share some of my experiences in using Therapeutic Touch with patients in the operating room.

Therapeutic Touch has been called a "healing meditation" (Peper and Ancoli, 1979). "Meditation is a key which opens the door to higher perceptions, unlocking the perfect wisdom in our hearts" (Pelletier, 1977). Some refer to it as prayer, listening to the voice within, awareness, and total relaxation. In the meditative state, the person may perform activities of daily living with a kind of attention that frees him from distractions. Thus, the practitioner of Therapeutic Touch benefits by being a channel for healing energies because the process of centering involves quieting the external stimuli and getting in touch with the stillness in oneself. Colleagues, co-workers, and patients also benefit, for this centered presence is felt by all around.

During the process of Therapeutic Touch, the healer is a channel for directing these energies to the person in need. Being a channel involves putting oneself in an egoless state. Thus, the healer gives up taking credit or taking responsibility for the success or nonsuccess of the healing process.

Using Therapeutic Touch during Local Anesthesia

During local procedures with the patient still awake, the consciousness of the patient can facilitate the effect of Therapeutic Touch. There is more time for contact with the person. In the role of circulating nurse, my responsibility is to monitor the patients' vital signs. This gives me more of an opportunity to be with the patients. Standing by the head of the patients, I have often seen the fear in their faces as they are separated from seeing what they are feeling behind the sterile drapes. Often, they do not know what to expect. At times simply informing the patient about what is happening or will happen next can help to relax the patient.

Deep breathing is also helpful. I gently place a hand on the patients' arm, shoulder, or forehead, just to let them know they are not alone. This physical touch must come from a reassuring, calm person, since our "vibes" are quickly picked up. While doing this I take deep breaths along with the patient, not only for demonstration, but also for my own relaxation and centering. I use this time to visualize calmness and peace, using my own symbols and colors. I then make the intent to be a channel for this healing energy and direct these energies to the patient through my hands. This can also be done without physical touch on my part. Making the intent to help and being centered and egoless makes this relationship a healing interaction.

Therapeutic Touch needs to be individualized for each patient and practitioner. For instance, to help me "center," I vary my visualizations of calmness and peace. I think of some familiar physical surroundings that make me feel calm, such as standing at the ocean's edge in the soft, warm, white sand, watching the waves break, and smelling the fresh salty air. Sometimes I am walking among the magnificent beauty of Mother Nature's forest, filled with the power and strength of the trees. I also instruct the patient to think back to a time, place, or experience that was peaceful for him or her. Together we do this while taking slow, deep breaths.

Some patients have been helped to relax by visualizing a white light coming in from the top of their heads, that fills their bodies with each breath. I may also suggest a blue light, as this is a cool, calming color. As the Therapeutic Touch practitioner I can be instrumental in facilitating that relaxed feeling by centering and feeling it inside myself and then directing this energy to the patient.

I would like to share with you an experience I had with a young woman patient. Ms. C was a very closed, tight, and frightened individual, as was evident in her diagnosis of ulcerative colitis. Her medical history included multiple hospitalizations and surgeries within the last couple of years. She was basically terrorized by the thought of another surgical procedure. Because of her numerous surgeries with general anesthetics within the last few months, this minor procedure was planned under a local anesthetic. She had been premedicated before coming to the OR as well as given a narcotic intravenously in the OR before the case was begun. Since her fears were very real, a most important part of my contact with her was to develop a trusting relationship and to instruct her. Deep breathing was used to relax her during the injections of local anesthetic. It was not easy to stay calm and centered myself, because of her hysteria. Verbal communication continued throughout most of our contact, and during this time I discovered that she was religious and believed in God. This helped me to develop a relaxation technique specifically for her. I instructed her to visualize a stream of white light, symbolic of God, coming in through the top of her head with each breath, and with each exhalation, to see the light radiate through her body. She talked about how singing made her happy, and she told me that she had written some gospel music. I had to ask her only once before her beautiful voice filled the OR suite. One song led to the next, and she kept on singing as if she was not having surgery at all. The surgeon, who also enjoys this kind of music, would join along with the songs that he knew. At the end everyone felt happy, especially the patient. She could hardly believe we were finished.

There are times when talking with the patient and being with him or her at the head of the table are impossible due to the type of surgery that is being performed. For instance, Mr. B was having a local surgical procedure on his nose and this meant that his upper torso, head, and arms were draped under the sterile field. The relaxation-breathing techniques were still possible; but since I could not get my hands on his arms, shoulders, or forehead, I went to his feet. Although relatively free of pain, his clinched fists, curled toes and tense leg muscles indicated his anxiety. With Mr. B's permission, I started giving him a foot massage. From my experience, rubbing or massaging of the feet is soothing and therapeutic. While doing this I was centered and directed healing energy to him.

Using Therapeutic Touch during General Anesthesia

The majority of surgical cases are done under general anesthesia, at which time I do not have as much opportunity to be with the patient. I take time, however, to help the anesthesiologist prepare the patient for induction. This gives me those few precious moments of contact with the patient. Being available to comfort the patients and helping them to go to sleep calmly and comfortably can be of great benefit postoperatively. From my experience, when a patient goes to sleep frightened and anxious, he/she usually wakes up that way in the Recovery Room. The opposite is also true. A patient who relaxes and welcomes the drug-induced sleep awakes less traumatically. During the operative procedure, although I may be across the room from the patient, I direct to him/her thoughts of peace and wholeness.

If time permits prior to induction, "unruffling the field" (Krieger, 1979, p. 55) can be helpful in producing a physiological relaxation. I tell the person that I have learned a technique that will help him/her to relax and I would like to use it. I inform patients that there is no physical touching and ask them to close their eyes. I stand on either side of the person. I move my hands, which are palm down and parallel to each other and to the patient, slowly over the patient's body from the head toward the feet. My hands are about four to six inches away from the body's surface. There is no need to uncover the patient. I go beyond the feet and shake my hands, as if shaking off water. This process is repeated again. While doing this, I feel in my hands sensations of heaviness, tingling, heat, or cold. These changes in the sensory cues of my hands are indications of the status of the patient's energy field. The reason for shaking my hands is to get rid of any "charges" I may have picked up while "unruffling" the patient's field. Most people sense this type of nonphysical stroking as being very soothing and conducive to relaxation. This physiological relaxation greatly benefits the induction of general anesthesia.

My experiences in the clinical setting of the OR with Therapeutic Touch have been special moments for me. They are the times I feel that I have done the most possible to help the patient, making my job as a nurse very fulfilling. Therapeutic Touch, as a useful adjunct to conventional methods in the operating room, represents the best of both worlds.

Bibliography

Krieger, D. *The Therapeutic Touch: how to use your hands to help or to heal.* Englewood Cliffs, N.J.: Prentice-Hall, 1979.

Pelletier, K. *Mind as healer, mind as slayer.* New York: Delta, 1977.

Peper, E. and Ancoli, S. Two endpoints of an EEG continuum of meditation—alpha/theta and fast beta. Appendix to D. Krieger, *The Therapeutic Touch: how to use your hands to help or to heal.* Englewood Cliffs, N.J.: Prentice-Hall, 1979.

Chapter 9

Pioneering Therapeutic Touch in Jail

Joey Upland

The Prison Environment

Jail is our democratic attempt to remove and dispose of the undesirable elements of our society. Contrary to popular belief, however, jail is a world that is not separate from "free" society. On a continuum from the most outstanding citizen, to the tax cheater, to the hit-and-run fender bender, to the street criminal, the line of freedom is drawn at jail. Most of us who live freely on one side of the line have judged that incarcerated persons naturally belong at the bottom of society, when, in fact, these are only the persons who were caught. The locked environment creates a concentrated collection of the poisons of the greater environment, and when one enters a jail, one is immediately hit with the intensity of this toxicity.

Although inmates are provided with basic food, clothing, shelter, and medical treatment, the lack of attention and denial of the needs for privacy, family, friends, personal possessions, and human touch prevents the release of these toxins. Frustrated needs and anger are often diverted into illness or further destructive behavior. Frequently, the nurse is the first person to be presented with the illness. Illness takes many forms in a prison environment, and it is important for the nurse-healer to understand the implication of this amidst the value judgments of the greater society.

Editing and input of vital energy by Ms. Ayumi Kie is gratefully acknowledged.

In prison, the main form of medical care for any form of disease is drug therapy. There are no other effective ways established to alleviate any tension or pain. Thus, drug habits formed outside of the jail are often desperately maintained within the jail, especially when it is the only support an inmate feels he has in surviving his stay. It is ironic that free drugs are provided for inmates jailed for drug-related crimes and that persons not on drugs prior to being jailed are very likely to be by the time they are released.

An inmate revealed to me that the three main preoccupations of a person doing time are planning further criminal activity, obtaining sex, and using drugs. There is a tight network among inmates that makes obtaining drugs and sex an expected part of prison life. For some inmates, jail is an opportunity to seek free drugs and medical care from doctors, dentists, and psychiatrists that would not necessarily be sought outside of jail. In addition to the drugs illegally obtained inside the jail, many inmates will use illness to obtain drugs through the medical staff. Through the jail grapevine, an inmate learns what symptoms to exhibit so that drugs are prescribed. The desperate manipulation, the con-games that are played, and the lengths to which an inmate will go to achieve these forms of release requires that the nurse maintain the strictest security procedures at all times. Moreover, one quickly becomes aware of the fact that many medical complaints are manipulative behavior designed to con the system. The nurse is required to determine the difference between a "real" illness and a "con" job.

The Nurse-Healer in the Prison Environment

Because any kind of loving touch that may soothe needs and prevent an inmate from further losing touch with basic humanness is suspect and absent in this environment, the nurse becomes the provider of basic human nurture for the inmate, whether in the form of dispensing pills or a healing touch. The qualities held by the nurse-healer are vital life sources for an inmate, and, indeed, providing a loving touch can be a very powerful instrument of healing. The daily living situation in the jail environment of disease, hatred, violence, apathy, depression, hopelessness, despair, manipulation, and self-destruction makes an inmate very sensitive and very vulnerable to any kind of touching. Thus, the simpler and clearer the interaction between the nurse-healer and inmate, the more therapeutic the touch seems to be. When the touch is administered in a specific caring manner it becomes profoundly therapeutic; when administered in a neglectful manner it is harmful.

Tools and machines normally used by nurses are considered weapons in jail. A woman inmate, for instance, took the clip used to fasten her ace bandage, broke it in half and slit her wrists. The necessity of strictly limiting and locking all her instruments brings the hands and heart of the nurse-healer into focal attention. They become the basic tools of administering care.

In this prison, certain routine functions are expected of the nurse. These include clearing a person to determine their fitness for custody, which may mean detoxifying alcoholics and drug addicts; managing flu or other epidemics; testing for tuberculosis; dispensing drugs; administering first aid treatments; treating emergencies such as assisting during a grand mal seizure or with a pregnant woman in labor; and running a clinic for the doctors and mental health staff. In this jail, nurses are on duty 24 hours a day. There are usually one or two nurses for 700 men and one nurse for 150 women. At night, there is one nurse for all of them. Receiving, triaging, and treating 850 persons in an ordinary environment is challenging; in a prison environment it is explosive. The fact that the majority of the inmates are ill in one way or another most of the time is only one aspect of this situation. The medical section of jail is considered the only neutral place where the inmates feel some of their needs are met; persons upholding custody accept this and assist in directing all such needs to nurses.

The Use of Therapeutic Touch in the Prison Environment

This is the environment within which I work as a nurse-healer. In the following paragraphs, I would like to describe how some of my experiences here have been humbling as well as richly rewarding.

Two inmates who were "trustees," or those with earned special privileges, requested healing during a brief conversation at pill call.

They had seen me using Therapeutic Touch with a deputy sheriff with a headache. I cleared arrangements and treated them both, behind bars. These trustees were also considered to be ringleaders of 45 men living in one side of medium security. The reactions were immediate and varied. Other inmates expressed fascination, awe, jealousy, and interest in being treated themselves. The deputies told me it was "impossible to have compassion" for these two "con men of con men" and doubted any change could occur. A sergeant worried that I could easily have been held hostage by these men and created serious security problems. A great level of trust had been established through the healing interaction, and when I informed the "trustees" that I could no longer treat them behind bars because of the security dangers, they responded with disappointment and protectiveness. They assured me that they would not have allowed anyone to harm me, and that anyone who attempted to would have to deal with them first. At their request I decided to treat them and others through healing at a distance. The negative reactions immediately subsided.

One of the "trustees" was a brilliant man who already had spent three years behind bars for his involvement in worldwide drug trafficking. It was his earnest desire to get out of the convict world, but it was difficult to do for one who had heavily invested in and whose lifestyle was amply supported by a vast network of contacts that is normally developed inside prison. He did not feel he had a viable alternative to turn to upon release. The relationship established through Therapeutic Touch allowed open and honest interactions to continue for several months. I treated him as time allowed and acted as a mirror, feeding back his own experiences, insights, and openings. He continually asked for assistance, and I treated him many times using Therapeutic Touch, providing trust, security, and mirrored feedback of his intentions. It was during these healings that he felt his "heart" had been healed to a degree enabling him to become a healer for other inmates inside the prison system. His life transformation continues in defiance of the dangers inherent in leaving the depths and entrenchment of prison life. He has indeed provided a respected life for himself, and he attributes the transition to the healing he received in jail.

The other "trustee" was also treated through distant healing. During his first weeks in jail he enjoyed his position of ringleader among the other inmates. During his trial, however, he became depressed, lost his gregarious spirit, and gained a great deal of weight. Using Therapeutic Touch for a few weeks, he regained his spirits and his original weight, and he hoped to return home soon. Then he was unexpectedly sentenced to psychiatric observation in a prison having a reputation for being a brutal concentration of habitual criminals. The day of his sentencing, he called his parents and found that his father had suffered a heart attack upon hearing the news of his son's sentence. That night, in a cage in the processing building, wearing only a prison jumpsuit, he asked a deputy sheriff to call and let me know he was leaving. I went to see him before he was transferred and this "con man's con man," rather than trying to save face among the other inmates, allowed me to see him silently crying. He told me that through our treatments he felt he had renewed strength to survive the pressures of prison life and to hold on to the hope of returning home to his parents. I continued healing him from a distance. He has since returned home, found a job, and is doing well.

I have learned through these two and many other relationships that compassion with the intent to heal must come from a strong belief system which views all humanity as interconnected. We are all human beings surviving together whether we are free or imprisoned, powerful or powerless, rich or poor, full of health and vitality or ridden with disease and afflicted with human weakness.

Acting on a "bleeding heart," especially in a jail environment, can be dangerous to the healer as well as the healee. The intense toxicity in the environment can easily flood the healer. Thus, in order to protect oneself, the healer must be grounded in an understanding of the process of Therapeutic Touch. He/she must know how to "center" or to remain in the "meditative state." The healer must be grounded in a strong belief system that does not allow this inmate to become emotionally attached to the healer and avoid taking responsibility for his/her own life.

Just as people naturally seek out the shade of a tree, inmates who truly need assistance will seek out the healer and opportunities will present themselves for healing. By being centered and grounded in the prison environment, a healer presents a powerful healing force. A simple procedure such as changing a bandage, touching an inmate with respect, and returning the trust placed in the healing interaction contains all the elements of the healing situation. Attention is focused on a wound which reflects the pain the person is suffering in jail and in life. If the wound can be treated with compassion, the healing will affect all levels of awareness.

I frequently changed the bandages on a 20-year-old woman who had been the subject of local public controversy. This woman was very nervous and was maintained on large amounts of drugs which she felt she needed. Her leg was recovering very slowly from a bad burn, and one day we decided to work with Therapeutic Touch. She was very excited when the flesh-colored wound that was open and weeping fluid covered over with new skin containing her normal black pigmentation within three days. Then escape charges, newspaper publicity, and a complex series of events resulted in an additional two years and eight months of sentencing for her. She came to me after her sentencing and asked me to help keep her from "going crazy." Her body trembled as she described her anguish in the courtroom and her life, revealing that in her adolescence she had been raped by three uncles and a cousin. I used Therapeutic Touch with her and then instructed her in facilitating the healing within herself. For the first time in months, her speech was not slurred, her gait was eased, and the dazed look on her face changed to that of a child. That night, she slept peacefully for the first time in years.

A jail environment fosters the festering of wounds suffered initially outside of jail. Wounds and illnesses are used as a means of releasing some of the toxicity suffered, but if in the process of discharge they are further infected or if the discharge is suppressed—by drugs or by being locked away—the process is further aggravated and healing is made more difficult. By treating not only the symptoms of a wound but the total persn, a deeper healing can occur from within and can extend out to the person.

The inmates frequently express appreciation for my helping them to laugh, saying that one smile does take away a lot of pain. Teaching visualizations, homework exercises, stress management skills, and health-maintaining habits gives additional support to the healing process. The healer in a jail environment extends light into darkness, facilitating inmates' sincere desires to redirect their lives. One such desire was shared by a woman inmate, J. G., in a poem entitled "Beyond":*

*Used with permission.

To go beyond is now my dream
To see the sights that others see
To smell the grass and taste the air
To see your eyes and show I care.
To go beyond these prison gates
*   and have you wash me clean of hate.*
To feel your arms and see the sun,
To be together as two are one.

Chapter 10

Self-Healing: Getting in Touch with Self to Promote Healing

Honore Fontes

Give a man a fish and you feed him for a day.
Teach a man to fish and you feed him for a
lifetime.

—Chinese proverb

My framework for healing or health promotion is to facilitate change in the direction of integration within the human field and greater synchrony of the field with its universal environment. Synchrony, as here used, is defined by Rogers (1970, p. 98) as "a function of the state of the human field at a specific point in space–time interacting with the environmental field at the same specified point in space–time."

Observations of other healers and my own healing interactions convince me that healing through Therapeutic Touch, group energy, healing at a distance, and self-healing are human potentials present, in varying degrees, in all individuals. I also believe that these healing potentials can be augmented through practice. As I continue to experiment with various forms of healing, my greatest strength seems to be in a meditative technique of self-healing, which I describe in this chapter.

The Process of Self-Healing

Although basically a healthy person, I am occasionally subject to sore throats and muscle spasms in my shoulders and at the base of my neck. The latter is almost always related to increased pressure at work or in my personal life. After several years, I am confident that by using the technique described below, I have facilitated healing and a remarkable decrease in duration and severity of these disease processes. The following steps describe my self-healing technique.

Intention

I sit in a quiet place with my eyes closed and my head supported, trying to be as comfortable and free from distraction as possible. I identify the place of my illness or discomfort, and I make the intention of mobilizing the healing forces within me.

Centering

I observe the sensation of air as it passes over my upper lip into my nostrils for a few seconds until my mind seems clear and I perceive a deep peace and calm.

Channeling

I believe there are two sources of healing energy. I visualize one stream of synchronizing, integrating energy pouring into me from the cosmos. I also visualize that part of my own energy field which is highly integrated and synchronous with the environment "influencing," or healing the relatively minor diseased part.

Visualization

I use visual imagery to aid me in self-healing. For example, when muscles of my shoulders have contracted, I visualize first the individual fibers relaxing and subsequently the entire muscle and muscle group relaxing and lengthening. When the contraction releases in my shoulder and neck, I actually have the sensation of my shoulders widening.

Breathing

I try to synchronize the healing process with my own respirations, for I believe that illness may be a deficit of *prana*, or life force (Krieger, 1972). I visualize the healing forces pouring into me from the cosmic sources as I inhale. During exhalation, I direct my own healing energies to my disease or discomfort, and expel disharmonious forces from my field.

Time

Often symptoms of a relatively minor ailment, such as I described, disappear after a single self-healing process. I allow approximately 15 to 20 minutes per session, but remain open to a sense of need to shorten or lengthen the process.

I recently suffered a severe traumatic injury and, although several months and much assistance from the therapeutic community and loving friends were required to accomplish the healing process, I used essentially the same technique at intervals. I healed faster than the schedule projected by the doctors and derived considerable comfort and relief of symptoms as well.

Closure

At the termination of each self-healing process I am aware of a feeling of gratitude for the healing resources available to me. Although on some occasions there is no immediate change, often I am aware that a perceptible change has occurred after only a single self-healing session.

Self-Healing: A Human Potential

Although I offer the above technique as I use it today, it is still in the process of evolution for me. Self-healing is a highly personal and dynamic experience. I would encourage interested persons to use my technique as a base, to explore the literature in the area, and then to listen carefully to their own personal responses. In this way they can develop a system of self-healing that is comfortable for them individually.

The concept of self-healing as an adjunct/alternative to Therapeutic Touch and other healing modalities is valuable for several reasons. Familiarity with self-healing provides the opportunity to move in the direction of independence and self-reliance. A goal of holistic health care is to move in the direction of greater personal responsibility. Ardell (1977, p. 97) writes: "It is essential that health education be targeted specifically on discovering and promulgating ways to motivate us to accept responsibility for our own health.. . ." Illich (1976), in a more extreme position, considers the health care delivery system and our dependence upon it so hopeless that he cautions: "Better health care will depend, not on some new therapeutic standard, but on the level of willingness and competence to engage in self-care." Another practical consideration is that a healer may not always be available. We often experience disease when we are alone. Skilled healers have many demands upon their time; it may be unnecessary to enlist assistance for ailments such as transient tension-related conditions or minor infections.

As the potential for self-healing emerged as my greatest strength, I began to consider its value as a potential in others. I continued to practice Therapeutic Touch on family and friends, but I began to explore their interest in learning the technique of self-healing. After counseling a few people who expressed an interest, several reported practicing the technique and having positive experiences. My 12-year-old son has been very open to my suggestions and uses some modification of the technique with his own disease. We communicate easily and quite naturally on the subject. If he has a minor physical complaint, a brief phrase from me, such as think good thoughts, serves as a reminder to do some self-healing. Often his next communication on the subject is to report the disappearance of symptoms.

Recently a friend sought advice on a stiff neck. We are both runners and the occasion was just before a race. I explained my technique for self-healing to her and, while she meditated on self-healing, simultaneously I did Therapeutic Touch. We both visualized streams of blue energy drawing the tension out of the muscles in her neck. She reported a definite relaxation of tension. After about 20 minutes she experienced significant relief and we were able to run successfully in the race.

For a variety of reasons, such as the severity of the condition or the individual's need to remain ill, not all disease processs are amenable to self-healing as described above. Persons who have become dependent on their symptoms in the past, but who seem to be in conflict about this and are looking for ways to greater independence, may be particularly open to trying self-healing techniques.

My experience with a person who suffered from a chronic colitis may illustrate this point. Initially I used Therapeutic Touch with some success. After each session the subject was relaxed and experienced relief from symptoms, but I was unable to perceive any lasting effect; his condition seemed relatively unchanged. I also wondered if I was feeding into manipulative dependency needs by working with him on a regular basis. In conversation I received clues that this person might be conflicted about the sick role and ready to assume greater responsibility for health. He was reading literature from the Theosophical Society and investigating various relaxation techniques. After we explored self-healing and visualization together, he was receptive to experimenting with meditation and self-healing. After many years of debilitating illness he now enjoys relatively good health.

I believe the word *heal* is not synonomous with the word *cure*. Movement in the direction of *diminished disease* seems to avoid that conflict. All persons can expect to experience the aging and dying processes. For those who believe that we are greater than and different from the sum of our parts, it is possible for the "holistic" self to transcend and move beyond the failure of the past. Individuals with life-threatening ailments often experience relief of symptoms and a sense of ease or peace, even though they are not "cured" and the dying process is imminent.

Conclusion

A variety of adjunctive healing practices which have been used throughout the history of man are being explored by modern medicine (*U.S. News and World Report*, 1979). Some of these healing modalities have been scientifically validated with research (Krieger, 1972; Krieger, Peper, and Ancoli, 1979). In this chapter I have suggested that self-healing is an alternative healing modality which may be used effectively alone or as an adjunct to Therapeutic Touch. Examples of this intervention indicate that a variety of persons, including the author, have received effective results from practice of self-healing techniques.

Bibliography

Ardell, D. B. *High level wellness*. Emmaus, Pa: Rodale Press, 1977.

Illich, I. *Medical nemesis*. New York: Random House, 1976.

Krieger, D. The response of in-vivo human hemoglobin to an active healing therapy by the direct laying-on of hands: a pilot study. *Human Dimensions*, 1972, *1*, 12–15.

Krieger, D. Therapeutic Touch: the imprimatur of nursing. *American Journal of Nursing*, 1975, *75*, 784–787.

Krieger, D., Peper, E., and Ancoli, S. Therapeutic Touch: searching for evidence of physiological change. *American Journal of Nursing*, 1979, *79*, 660–662.

Rogers, M. E. *An introduction to the theoretical basis of nursing*. Philadelphia: F. A. Davis, 1970.

U.S. News and World Report. Science takes a new look at faith healing. *U.S. News and World Report*. February 12, 1979, 68–69.

Chapter 11

Scientific Medicine and Therapeutic Touch

Martin Proudfoot

[An] important principle is the laying-on of hands—a practice that is rapidly atrophying because physicians are too busy with the laying-on of tools.

—B. Lown, M.D.
(Lown & Segal, 1978, p. 60)

Introduction

Health professionals may find "laying-on of hands" offensive to their training in science. Therapeutic Touch may be considered the same as hocus-pocus by these individuals. This chapter is a response to such a point of view.

There are three main points to be made: (1) Only a small proportion of medical practice is scientific. (2) There is a theoretical basis and scientific evidence for Therapeutic Touch. (3) There are specific indications for Therapeutic Touch in current medical practice.

Advocates of science, including physicians and nurses, tend to regard their own practices as scientific and legitimate and alternative types of therapy as unscientific, fraudulent, and incompatible with orthodox medicine. This assumption is inherent in a question often asked by medical colleagues: "If you had a cancer of your colon, who would you go to: a surgeon to cut it out, or a 'faith healer'?" My answer is as surprising to them as they think it untenable: I would do both.

The opportunity for alternative forms of therapy to develop occurs only because curative therapy, scientific or otherwise, does not exist. It is reasonable for patients to seek other modalities when scientific medicine offers only empiric palliation.

Scientific Medicine

Limitations

Undeniable advances in treatment have been made through experimental research in surgical techniques, antibiotic therapy, and public health practices. Scientific therapies are the most reliable and effective treatments. Nonetheless, deductions from experiments have not proceeded to a complete and exhaustive characterization of reality.

Investigators' understanding of normal anatomy and physiology is still incomplete. Old concepts are retracted and new theories are offered. For example, the human nervous system has been classically divided into two parts: the voluntary and the autonomic. Recent investigations have found that not only is what was thought to be autonomic not involuntary (Green and Green, 1977, pp. 21–41), but there is a third division of the nervous system, the neuroendocrine, which was previously unrecognized (Guillemin, 1978). Without thorough knowledge of normal human structure and function, it is impossible to understand abnormal states in disease, and rational therapy of such illness is literally beyond physicians' comprehension.

The applications of the scientific method in human studies has limitations in itself. Experimental studies of some experiences are impossible. For example, observation of perceptions of individuals in near death experiences is implausible. Disciplined investigators recognize that there is a vast range of phenomena to which the scientific method cannot be applied. Experimentation is not an all-inclusive tool for characterizing all events in reality. Therefore, it cannot be relied upon as the sole source of legitimate information. The lack of scientific validation does not falsify an experience, it only means that the event is outside the domain of science.

Ethical considerations preclude strict clinical research. Scientific investigation does not supersede the interests of the patient. Clinical trials have been discontinued prior to an uncontroversial conclusion when preliminary data indicated patients were suffering under the experimental design of the study (University Group Diabetes Program, 1970). Analogously, physicians in clinical practice treat the patient as well as possible in spite of the lack of scientific substantiation of the therapy.

The scientific method is cumbersome. The legitimate clinical study is prospective, double-blind, and match-controlled. Meeting these requirements is expensive. For example, in regard to whether "tight" control of the blood sugar with insulin in diabetes is beneficial, one investigator (Bressler, Cahill, and Siperstein, 1978) says that the research is unlikely to be done because the cost is prohibitive. Even when the methodology is available, science may be unable to supply the answers because doing so is impractical.

Science does not have a monopoly on the truth. Investigators assume that the laws of nature that they characterize have existed prior to discovery. While the scientific method is a common tool for the elucidation of nature, it is not the only one. Whether a person undertakes tedious measurements and calculations to become aware that the moon varies in relation to the tides or whether a person sits on the seashore and intuitively becomes conscious of the relations between the moon and tides does not alter the truth of the fact. Experience and intuition do not replace the reliability of the scientific method for many individuals; nonetheless, in areas that have not been characterized experimentally, experience and intuition may be all that is available.

Empiric Therapy

There are many diseases that are poorly understood by investigators and clinicians. These include the widespread diseases of arteriosclerosis, cancer, diabetes, and arthritis, to cite a few. Countless numbers of people suffer and die of diseases that are incurable by scientific knowledge and technique.

Empiric therapies, inside and outside the orthodox health professions, are considered alternatives when no curative therapy exists. Treatment is based on what works. Characterization of the pathological process is incomplete. Understanding about how and why the therapy works is tenuous. What specific effect the treatment has on the disease itself may be unknown. Insulin therapy in diabetes is an example. Whether "tight" control of the blood sugar decreases the incidence of diabetic complications of retinopathy, angiopathy, and neuropathy is a highly debated question. Schools of diabetic specialists take sides on the issue. There has been no experimental study in humans to establish the answer (Bressler, Cahill, and Siperstein, 1978). The frequency and dose of insulin injections in diabetic therapy is not scientifically established. It is empiric, based on the experience of the physician as to what works.

It is legitimate to offer empiric treatment. However, empiric therapies are not necessarily rational or strictly scientific. In fact, only a small proportion of current medical practice is scientific (Stead, 1979). Therapeutic modalities should not be excluded from health practice on the basis of lack of thorough scientific substantiation. A therapy that works for some people and has little risk of unwanted effects is generically similar to a large proportion of current medical practice. Therapeutic Touch is one modality that has increasing experimental validation and benefits diseased individuals.

Therapeutic Touch

The theoretical basis, scientific evidence, procedure, and applications of Therapeutic Touch are elaborated in separate chapters in this book. I wish to make a few comments to the individual with strict scientific training.

Theoretical Basis

A significant point to be emphasized is that there is no appeal to miracles. No reference is made to a supernatural suspension of universal law. On the contrary, Therapeutic Touch is derived from theories of natural law that are in effect continuously, but unrecognized by many people.

My understanding, stated briefly, is that there is a universal life force or energy that is the primordial constituent of the human body. It is somewhat like electromagnetic energy, except that electron flow would be considered extremely coarse compared to this universal energy. While my understanding is limited, I think of it as a flow of energy that follows the branches of the nervous system from the brain to the peripheral nerves. Emanations of the energy exist in a field about the body (Govinda, 1969, pp. 150–154). This energy flows from one individual to another. A meditative state of awareness facilitates the flow.

Using the hands as focal points, this essential energy passes from the healthy person to the ill person during the process of Therapeutic Touch. The patient's energy system is thus augmented and balanced. It is assumed that the disease will be overcome when the energy flow is returned to its healthy, natural state (Krieger, 1975).

Scientific Evidence

Karagulla (1967, pp. 123–146) studied individuals who claimed to perceive energy flow in the human body and found that descriptions of patients' diseases were consistent with the medical record of physicians. Benson (1975) showed that a meditative state of mind can result in a beneficial physiological effect called the relaxation response.

The recent explosion of research in endorphins (endogenous morphine-like substances) is relevant to Therapeutic Touch. Small-chain polypeptide molecules produced by the human body have tens of times more potency than morphine in its analgesic and other narcotic effects (Terenius, 1978). This endogenous activity can be reversed by administration of the narcotic antagonist naloxone. Acupuncture analgesia can be reversed by naloxone and presumably works through an activation of endorphins (Mayer, Price, and Rafii, 1977). Studies in humans have shown that the placebo effect of analgesia can be reversed by the administration of naloxone (Levine, Gordon, and Fields, 1978). One possible explanation of these data is that the expectation of analgesia in the patient activates the endorphin system. State of mind may possibly result in the very specific molecular activity of endorphins. I expect that the analgesic effect of Therapeutic Touch is reversible by naloxone, thereby implicating an activation of endorphins as a mechanism through which Therapeutic Touch works. This experiment should be done in the near future.

Experimentation in other sciences is pertinent. The discipline of physics has experienced a revolution of previously imponderable proportions since the turn of this century. The universal characterization of the motion of matter found previously in Newtonian mechanics has been replaced by Einsteinian relativity. Investigations of subnuclear particles have led to expressions of their activity that are similar to the tenets of Eastern mystics (Capra, 1975). The reverberations of these findings in the pure sciences have not yet been fully recognized in the life sciences. It is my opinion that medical science is beginning a revolution of parallel proportion and effect. The work in Therapeutic Touch, endorphins, and neuroendocrinology may culminate in an understanding of the power of the brain and mind that will drastically change scientific medicine.

Indications and Results

Therapeutic Touch may be applied to almost any ill person. This is because Therapeutic Touch is a health-oriented rather than disease-oriented therapy. Most interventions prescribed by physicians are disease specific. Such measures are intended to alter the disease process and/or the body's response to illness. Medicines inhibit "causes" of illness such as bacteria; or they may compensate for diseased organs by inducing counterbalancing responses in other organs, or drugs may suppress the disease process and/or the body's response. Surgery removes or reconstructs pathological anatomy. Rarely is medicine or surgery able to intensify normal physiology. Therapeutic Touch works by enhancing natural body function. By augmenting and balancing the flow of the primordial energy, the body's systems are returned to a healthy state. During the assessment phase of Therapeutic Touch, an awareness of the disturbance of energy flow is sought. During the treatment phase, Therapeutic Touch is done in such a way as to return the poorly functioning parts of the body to normal balance. This process can be applied to almost any ill person and is therefore not disease specific.

Therapeutic Touch is indicated as an adjunctive, rather than definitive, therapy. The associated modalities may be medicines, surgery, or a combination of various interventions. Since Therapeutic Touch is an adjunctive measure, medical evaluation is a routine prerequisite. I know of no practitioner who does not recommend or require examination by a physician when significant disease is present in the patient.

As an adjunctive therapy, Therapeutic Touch does not claim to alter the prognosis in disease. Psychological and physiological effects occur via this intervention, but these may not result in a beneficial change in the course of the disease. In my experience, approximately 70 percent of individuals receive the short- or long-term effect of a decrease in their disease symptomatology. When long-term results are noted, the disease is usually one with a variable prognosis, such as asthma, epilepsy, emphysema, or lupus erythematosis. Individuals with diseases of universally dismal prognosis treated with Therapeutic Touch usually die as predicted by their physicians. It is important that practitioners let their patients know that an adjunctive modality, not a cure or a miracle, is being offered.

Because Therapeutic Touch is given in the midst of other therapeutic events, the ultimate outcome for the patient is influenced by multiple factors. The relationship between the practitioner and the patient is significant. The expectation and activity of the client are factors influencing the outcome. I do not mean to imply here that patients must believe in Therapeutic Touch in order to benefit from it. Indeed, some observers note that an open mind of accepting whatever happens, and specifically not expecting a cure, is associated with a better result (Kunz, 1978).

When the patient's debilitated resources prevent him or her from taking part in treatment, Therapeutic Touch can be utilized as a purely therapist-centered intervention, i.e., the practitioner performs the beneficial activity. Nonetheless, practitioners recognize the important principle that the patient is responsible for his own disease. Optimal effects result when Therapeutic Touch is combined with client-centered modalities in which the patient undertakes the work of treatment under the instruction of the therapist. It is my opinion that the comprehensive therapeutic plan that includes meditation, visualization, exercise, diet, and adjustment in life-style, as well as Therapeutic Touch, will result in beneficial changes in prognosis for patients with chronic and terminal diseases.

Specific indications for Therapeutic Touch include acute and chronic pain. Pain unrelieved by injectable narcotics has responded to Therapeutic Touch (Krieger, 1978). Hypertension responds to this intervention. It is expected that Therapeutic Touch would be useful in psychosomatic diseases including acute or chronic anxiety and/or depression, asthma with significant emotional component, low-back-pain syndrome, and peptic ulcer disease. In the terminally ill, practitioners of Therapeutic Touch have been involved in a process that has allowed grace and dignity to the dying. Helping patients to die in this manner may be counted as a "success story" because the individuals were able to accept their own deaths peacefully without fear and pain (Krieger, 1978).

Benefit-to-Risk Ratio

When no curative therapy exists, it is necessary to choose among various palliative measures. A significant consideration is the benefit-to-risk ratio; the likely benefits of any intervention must be weighed against the possible risks. Most medicinal and surgical therapies have definite risks involved in their use. The molecular or surgical alteration of human physiology can rarely be done without impending harm.

There is essentially no risk to using Therapeutic Touch. Enhancement, rather than alteration, of natural bodily function is not likely to result in complications. It is possible to make patients acutely uncomfortable with pain, nausea, etc., when Therapeutic Touch is administered by poorly trained practitioners. However, no long-term complications have been seen with its use.

When curative therapy does not exist and definitive treatment is not entirely satisfactory to the patient or physician, Therapeutic Touch represents an ideal adjunctive modality because of the large margin of safety associated with its use.

Conclusion

Scientific therapeutics are inadequate to cure a wide range of disease. Hence, a large proportion of current medical treatment is empiric palliation. Therapeutic Touch is generically similar to this practice. A theoretical basis has increasing scientific support. Therapeutic Touch is an extremely safe adjunctive modality indicated in patients with a wide variety of acute, chronic, and terminal diseases.

Bibliography

Benson, H. *The relaxation response.* New York: William Morrow, 1975; Avon, 1976.

Bressler, R., Cahill, Jr., G.F. and Siperstein, M.D. *Controversies in Diabetes: UGDP, DKA, Glucose Control.* Panel discussion at meeting of the American College of Physicians, Boston, Massachusetts, Spring, 1978.

Capra, F. *The tao of physics.* Berkeley: Shambhala, 1975.

Govinda, L.A. *Foundations of Tibetan mysticism.* New York: Samuel Weiser, 1969.

Green, E. and Green, A. *Beyond biofeedback.* New York: Dell, 1977.

Guillemin, R. Peptides in the brain: the new endocrinology of the neuron. *Science,* 1978, *202,* 390–402.

Karagulla, S. *Breakthrough to creativity.* Santa Monica, Calif.: De Vorss, 1967.

Krieger, D. Therapeutic Touch: the imprimatur of nursing. *American Journal of Nursing,* 1975, *75,* 784–787.

Krieger, D. Informal presentation at the Invitational Therapeutic Touch Healers' Workshop, Eastsound, Washington, June, 1978.

Kunz, D. Informal presentation at the Invitational Therapeutic Touch Healers' Workshop, Eastsound, Washington, June, 1978.

Levine, J. D., Gordon, N. C. and Fields, H. L. The mechanism of placebo analgesia. *Lancet,* 1978, *ii,* 654–657.

Lown, B. and Segal, J. Post-MI care: How to manage your patients' arrhythmias. *Modern Medicine,* 1978, September 30–October 15, 60–77.

Mayer, D. J., Price, D. D. and Rafii, A. Antagonism of acupuncture analgesia in man by the narcotic antagonist naloxone. *Brain Research,* 1977, *121,* 368–372.

Stead, E. A., Jr. Growing holistic doctors. *American Holistic Medicine,* 1979, *1,* 7–11.

Terenius, L. Endogenous peptides and analgesia. *Annual Review of Pharmacology and Toxicology,* 1978, *18,* 189–204.

University Group Diabetes Program. A study of the effects of hypoglycemic agents on vascular complications in patients with adult-onset diabetes. Part I: Design, methods, baseline characteristics. Part II: Mortality results. *Diabetes,* 1970, *19* (supplement 2), 747–829.

Chapter 12

The Effects of Therapeutic Touch on Anxiety Level of Hospitalized Patients

Patricia Heidt

Illness and hospitalization are often accompanied by an increase in the state of anxiety. Such feelings of tension interfere with the benefits to be derived from rest, a prescription given frequently to patients during all stages of illness. Deep rest and relaxation allow the body's constricted organs to assume their natural and balanced functioning (Hartman, 1973) and indeed are necessary for the organism's survival. The purpose of this research is to study the effects of therapeutic touch (Krieger, 1973) on the anxiety level of hospitalized patients.

Theoretical Background

The early research of Cannon (1914) described anxiety primarily as a sympathetic nervous system reaction. Gellhorn and Kiely (1972) presents evidence that it is the simultaneous functioning of both the parasympathetic and sympathetic nervous systems which destroys their reciprocal and balanced function and produces a state of anxiety. Research on subjects who meditate indicates that such a practice

Copyright (in press), American Journal of Nursing Company. Reproduced, with permission, from *Nursing Research*.

may produce a shift in this sympathetic-parasympathetic balance.

These physiological changes have been described as the "relaxation response " (Benson, Beary, and Carol, 1974). In an investigation of 36 subjects practicing transcendental meditation the major elements of the relaxation response occurred. Continuous monitoring of the subjects indicated that during the meditation period there were decreases in oxygen consumption, carbon dioxide elimination, heart rate, respiratory rate, and arterial blood lactate. The electroencephalographic records showed an increase in alpha waves and accompanying theta wave activity. Galvanic skin responses showed marked increases; there was slight increase in skeletal blood flow, while rectal temperature remained unchanged.

Research on Therapeutic Touch indicates the potential of this intervention for eliciting in the subject a state of physiological relaxation. In laboratory experimentation both the healer and healees were monitored on two consecutive days. The electroencephalographic and electromyographic records, galvanic skin response, temperature, and heart rate indicated that subjects were in a relaxed state with "high abundance of large amplitude alpha activity with both the eyes open and eyes closed state." Subjects also reported that during Therapeutic Touch they were relaxed (Krieger, Peper, and Ancoli, 1979).

This relaxation response is explained in Krieger's research (1975). She states that in the first phase of Therapeutic Touch, the person in the role of healer "centers" him/herself. The conciousness of the person intervening with Therapeutic Touch is "meditative." In this centered state the healer becomes aware of self as an open system of energies and concentrates attention on directing this energy to assist the person in need.

All living systems are vibrating fields of energy, sending and receiving information from the environment surrounding them (Tiller, 1977; Burr, 1972; Rogers, 1970; Ravitz, 1970). It is suggested that, through a continuous interchange of their fields during intervention by Therapeutic Touch, the ill person's energy field tends to become more like that of the healthy person, somewhat analogous to "electron transfer resonance" (Krieger, 1974). Through this field repatterning the healee's own self-healing mechanisms are stimulated and the ability to regulate the many functions in his/her living system is enhanced.

It is this factor of conscious use of self in patient interaction toward which research in Therapeutic Touch is directed. Krieger (1973) postulates that all nurse–patient interactions have the potential to be healing interactions. By this is meant that healing is a natural potential within all health professionals—all persons—which becomes actualized when the intention to help or heal the ill person is present. It is this motivation to help or heal and to understand the dynamics involved which changes a routine interaction into a healing or therapeutic interaction.

Historically, nursing is a profession in which a significant portion of its major functions is carried out through touching patients. When touch itself is introduced consciously and appropriately into the nurse–patient interaction, research indicates that it may facilitate the communication process, decrease levels of anxiety, and reinforce a component of security and warmth in the dyadic relationship (Weiss, 1979; McCorkle, 1974; Barnett, 1972; Rubin, 1963). Other studies demonstrate that routine clinical procedures, including the nurse's touch of the patient, effect important changes in the patient's heart rate, heart rhythm, and frequency of ectopic beats (Mills et al., 1976; Lynch et al., 1974a, 1974b).

Definition of Terms

This research employs four definitions:

A-State Anxiety

A transitional emotional state of the human organism that varies in intensity and fluctuates over time, A-State anxiety is differentiated from A-Trait anxiety in that the latter is defined as a relatively stable personality trait, characterized by feelings of diffuse apprehension and proneness to experience stressful events (Spielberger, 1966). The A-State anxiety score will be measured by the Self-Evaluation Questionnaire, Form x-1, as developed by Spielberger, Gorsuch, and Lushene (1970). It is administered pre- and post-intervention.

Therapeutic Touch

This is a derivative of laying-on of hands in that it uses the hands to direct excess body energies from a person playing the role of healer to another for the purpose of helping or healing that individual (Krieger, 1973). Although derived from the laying-on of hands, it differs from it in that Therapeutic Touch is not performed within a religious context. The person in the role of healer does the act of Therapeutic Touch while in a meditative state and is motivated by an interest in the needs of the patient (Krieger, 1975).

Casual Touch

This is an intervention in which the nurse takes the subject's apical and radial pulse, as well as the pedal pulse rate in both feet.

No Touch

In this intervention the nurse sits beside the subject and talks with him/her without any touching during this time. Two questions serve as an interview guide: (1) Can you tell me how you are feeling today? (2) How do you feel you're responding to your treatment?

The hypotheses tested are: (1) In subjects receiving intervention by Therapeutic Touch, there is a reduction in posttest A-State anxiety scores. (2) There is a greater reduction in A-State anxiety scores in subjects receiving intervention by Therapeutic Touch than in subjects receiving intervention by Casual Touch. (3) There is a greater reduction in A-State anxiety scores in subjects receiving intervention by Therapeutic Touch than in those subjects receiving intervention by No Touch.

Method

Subjects

The sample was composed of 90 volunteer subjects (27 women and 63 men), hospitalized on a cardiovascular unit of a general hospital in New York City. Subjects were limited to persons between ages 21 and 65 who were able to read and complete the English version of the Self-Evaluation Questionnaire (Spielberger, Gorsuch, Lushene, 1970). Subjects were excluded if neurological impairment made them unable to feel the touch of the nurse, or if the degree of their illness made them unable to participate for the length of the time needed in the research.

The mean age of the subjects in the total sample ($n = 90$) was 50.9 years of age, S.D. 11.3, with a range of 25 to 65 years. The three experimental groups were similar in mean age, standard deviations, and age range. Examination of demographic data (Table 1) indicates that the three groups were also very similar in the categories of ethnicity and sex. There was a slightly greater percentage of subjects who reported their religious background as Catholic in the No Touch group. The percentage of patients admitted for myocardial infarctions was greater in the Therapeutic Touch and Casual Touch groups. In the No Touch group there was a higher percentage of patients admitted for Tests/Observation and for preoperative open heart surgery.

Instruments

The Self-Evaluation Questionnaire, Form x-1 (Spielberger, Gorsuch, Lushene, 1970) was used to measure the degree of A-State anxiety pre- and post-intervention. The A-State scale consists of 20 statements that ask the subjects to describe how they feel at a particular moment in time. Subjects rate themselves on a four-point scale of increasing intensity.

Typical items in the A-State scale are "I feel nervous, I feel content, I am relaxed, I am jittery." To reduce the potential influence of an acquiescence set on the response, ten items in the A-State scale are scored directly and ten are reversed.

Normative data for patient populations are based on a sample of 446 neuropsychiatric patients and 161 general medical-surgical patients. In the neuropsychiatric population, on the A-State scale, the mean was 47.74, S.D. 13.24. Mean age for patients was 43 and mean educational level was tenth grade. In the general medical-surgical population, on the A-State scale the mean was 42.38, S.D. 13.24. Mean age and educational levels were 55 years and tenth grade (Spielberger, Gorsuch, Lushene, 1970).

The A-State scale was also validated with 197 undergraduate stu-

TABLE 1. Descriptive Statistics and Characteristics of the Three Experimental Groups as Reported on Personal Data Sheet*

Variable	Percentage of Therapeutic Touch†	Percentage of Casual Touch†	Percentage of No Touch†
Sex			
Male	70.0	65.5	70.0
Female	30.0	34.5	30.0
Ethnicity			
Black	16.7	10.3	13.3
White	83.3	86.2	80.0
Hispanic		3.5	3.3
Other			3.3
Religious Background			
Protestant	30.0	27.6	26.7
Roman Catholic	53.3	51.7	70.0
Jewish	13.3	20.7	
Other	3.3		3.3
Reason for Hospitalization			
Arrhythmia	10.0	6.9	3.3
Postoperative Open Heart	26.7	13.8	26.7
Preoperative Open Heart	13.3	13.8	20.0
Myocardial Infarction	26.7	27.6	13.3
Angina	13.3	17.2	3.3
Tests/Observation		6.9	23.3
Other	10.0	13.8	11.1
Practice of Meditation			
Yes	6.7	13.8	10.0
No	93.3	86.2	90.0
Practice of Relaxation			
Yes	3.3	6.9	
No	96.7	93.1	100.0

*N = 30 for each of the three groups.
†Percentages are reported to the nearest tenth.

dents under four experimental conditions. The first condition (NORMAL) occurred at the beginning of the testing session. Following a ten-minute period of relaxation (RELAX), a second administration took place. Following this, students began to work on another test, and they were interrupted after ten minutes for the third administration of the scale (EXAM). A final administration followed immediately after they watched a stressful movie (MOVIE). The means, standard deviations, and alpha reliability coefficients for the four conditions indicate the following results for men (n = 109):

1. MOVIE: Mean 50.03, S.D. 12.48, Alpha 4;
2. EXAM: Mean 43.01, S.D. 9.57, Alpha 0.89;
3. NORMAL: Mean 36.99, S.D. 9.57, Alpha 0.89;
4. RELAX: Mean 32.70, S.D. 9.02, Alpha 0.89.

Results for women (n = 88) are:

1. MOVIE: Mean 60.94, S.D. 11.99, Alpha 0.93;
2. EXAM: Mean 43.69, S.D. 11.59, Alpha 0.93;
3. NORMAL: Mean 37.24, S.D. 10.27, Alpha 0.91;
4. RELAX: Mean 29.60, S.D. 6.91, Alpha 0.83.

These results indicate that the MOVIE condition was more upsetting for women, and the RELAX condition more effective in reducing their level of A-State intensity. The suggestion was made that either women were more emotionally labile than male subjects or they were "more willing to report their feeling" (Spielberger, Gorsuch, Lushene, 1970, p.11).

Test–retest reliability for A-State scales were (men, n = 88): .33 (one-hour time lapse), 0.54 (20-day time lapse), and 0.33 (104-day time lapse). Results for women (n = 109) were similar. Given the transitory nature of anxiety states, measures of internal consistency, such as Alpha coefficient, provide a more meaningful index of reliability of A-State scales than test–retest conditions (Spielberger, Gorsuch, Lushene, 1970).

It is recommended that the A-State scale be given on each occasion for which a measure of change is needed. Studies in which the A-State subscale has been repeated within a short span of time indicate that this repeated usage has led to greater differentiation among subjects. Other studies utilizing this procedure also indicate that there has been no significant influence on test scores through frequent repetition of the questionnaire (Spielberger, Gorsuch, and Lushene, 1970, p. 4).

The Posttest Patient Interview Form consisted of five questions asked of the subject by the research assistant at the end of the period of research. The purpose of the interview was to collect verbal information on the feelings and thoughts of the subjects about the intervention they received.

Procedure

The setting for the research was in the hospital room of the subject. All subjects who participated were in semiprivate rooms. Curtains were drawn around the subject's area to ensure some degree of privacy.

The investigator and a research assistant consulted with the head nurse of the cardiovascular unit for the purpose of selecting subjects who met the limitations of the research. They then met with each subject individually, offered an explanation for the purpose of the research, and elicited from the subject whether he/she was interested in participating in the research. The investigator left the subject's room. The research administrator administered a Self-Evaluation Questionnaire. It was collected after 10 minutes.

The research assistant left the subject's room and scored the questionnaire. She assigned the subject to one of the three intervention groups on the basis of matching scores. She then informed the principal investigator to which group the subject was assigned and a five-minute intervention was administered by the principal investigator. Group A received intervention by Therapeutic Touch, Group B received intervention by Casual Touch, and Group C received intervention by No Touch.

All subjects were in a sitting position, either in a chair at their bedside or in their beds. All interventions were administered between 11:00 A.M. and 12:00 noon, a time when most treatments and other activities had been completed. All interventions were administered by the principal investigator, who is a registered nurse and has been taught by Kunz and Krieger to administer Therapeutic Touch. She has extensive background in psychiatric-mental health settings and is also qualified to administer the No Touch intervention.

Prior to each intervention, an explanation of the activity was offered to each subject. For subjects receiving intervention by Therapeutic Touch (Group A), the following explanation was given:

> I am studying how nurses use their hands to assess and treat areas of physical discomfort in their patients. I am going to use my hands and pass them over your body in a way that has been taught to me.

The following explanation was given to subjects receiving intervention by Casual Touch (Group B):

> I am studying how nurses use their hands to assess and treat areas of physical discomfort in their patients. I am going to take your pulse over your heart and at your wrist, and near both ankles. This is going to take longer than usual because it is part of a research project. This does not mean that there is anything wrong; it is simply part of a standardized procedure.

Subjects receiving intervention by No Touch (Group C) received this explanation:

> I am studying how nurses assess and treat physical discomfort in their patients. I am going to spend some time talking with you about how you are feeling today. Can you tell me how you are feeling right now?

At the end of the intervention time, the investigator left the subject's room. The research assistant then readministered the A-State Self-Evaluation Questionnaire (Spielberger, Gorsuch, Lushene, 1970). At the end of the ten minutes, she picked up the completed questionnaire and asked the subject to respond verbally to questions on the Posttest Patient Interview. The time of the research period for most subjects was 25 to 35 minutes. Subjects who could not complete the procedure as outlined above were eliminated from the research.

Intervention Groups

The process of Therapeutic Touch has been described as a "healing meditation" (Krieger, Peper, Ancoli, 1979) because the person in the role of healer enters a state of consciousness described as "meditative" to administer this treatment. The interventions of Casual Touch and No Touch differ in that the state of consciousness or awareness in which they are performed is the "ordinary" state of awareness. Tart (1975, 1969) in explaining these differences writes that the usual state of awareness in which the individual conducts his/her daily activities is but one state of consciousness to which he/she has access. Given the proper motivation and/or education, individuals may enter other states of consciousness. When they do this, they feel a "qualitative shift" in their pattern of mental functioning, i.e., they become aware of a noticeable change or difference in their mental operations (Tart, 1975, p. 3).

Thus, the three interventions of Therapeutic Touch, Casual Touch, and No Touch were distinct and different interventions when described in terms of the practitioner's state of consciousness during which they were administered. The following operational definitions describe the three interventions from this point of view:

Therapeutic Touch

Intervention by Therapeutic Touch consists of the following operational steps. During the process the nurse:

1. Makes the intention mentally to assist the subject therapeutically.
2. Centers herself in an act of self-relatedness and becomes aware of herself as an open system of energies in constant flux.
3. Moves the hands over the body of the subject from head to feet, attuning to the condition of the subject by becoming aware of changes in sensory cures in the hands
4. Redirects areas of accumulated tension in the subject's body by movement of the hands
5. Concentrates her attention on the specific direction of these energies, using her hands as focal points
6. Directs this energy to the subject by placing hands on the solar plexus area of the body (just above the waist) and leaves them in this area for approximately 90 seconds.

The total time for this intervention is five minutes.

Casual Touch

Intervention by Casual Touch consists of the following operational steps. During the process the nurse:

1. Focuses her attention on placing a stethoscope on the subject's chest area; counts the apical pulse rate by use of a watch for one minute and records it
2. Focuses her attention on locating the radial pulse with her

fingers on the subject's left wrist; counts the pulse rate by use of a watch for one minute and records it

3. Focuses her attention on locating the pedal pulse with her fingers on the subject's left ankle area; counts the pulse rate for one minute by use of a watch and records it

4. Focuses her attention on locating the pedal pulse with her fingers on the subject's right ankle area; counts the pulse rate for one minute by use of a watch and records it.

The total time for this intervention is five minutes.

No Touch

Intervention by No Touch consists of the following operational steps. During the process the nurse:

1. Focuses her attention on the subject and asks, "Can you tell me how you are feeling today?"

2. Focuses her attention on the subject's reply and her internal reaction to these statements

3. Focuses her attention on how the subject's body is corresponding to verbal comments, and makes a decision to (a) clarify any of the subject's comments she does not understand, and/or (b) ask for further description of the subject's response

4. Focuses her attention on the subject's reply and her internal reaction to these statements

5. Redirects her attention to asking the subject, "How do you feel you are responding to your treatment?"

6. Repeats steps 2, 3, and 4.

The total time for this intervention is five minutes.

Results and Discussion

Hypothesis One

Differences between pre- and posttest mean scores and adjusted mean scores on the Self-Evaluation Questionnaire for the three intervention groups is presented in Table 2. In the group of subjects re-

TABLE 2. Means, Standard Deviations, and Adjusted Means of A-State Anxiety in the Three Experimental Groups

	Pretreatment		Posttreatment		Adjusted Means
	Mean	S.D.	Mean	S.D.	
Therapeutic Touch	41.77	11.16	34.87	39.85	34.45
Casual Touch	40.52	11.97	38.79	13.47	39.20
No Touch	41.13	14.87	40.97	14.79	40.97

ceiving intervention by Therapeutic Touch, a comparison of pre- and posttest mean scores, using a correlated t ratio, revealed a highly significant difference (t (29) $= -4.88$, $p < 0.001$). Subjects in this group did have a decrease in anxiety supporting the first hypothesis.

In the Posttest Patient Interview, these subjects related the experience of intervention by Therapeutic Touch to feelings of relaxation and sleep by the following verbal comments: "I feel more calm; I feel tensionless; I feel restful; I feel like I was in another world with no noise and very quiet." Six subjects related the feeling to sleep, such as, "I feel like dozing off; I could go to sleep now; I felt peaceful and nearly went off to sleep." Others spoke about emotional rest, such as, "She gave me peace of mind; I felt like my problems went away for a while; I felt more cheerful; My problems are still there, but I don't feel worried." In written comments made by the research assistant, five patients were found "dozing, with eyes closed, or sleeping"; three patients were reluctant to fill out the questionnaire again because they felt "sleepy."

Hypothesis Two

Table 3 shows that the analysis of covariance comparing the Therapeutic Touch group with the Casual Touch group resulted in F

TABLE 3. Analysis of Covariance for A-State Anxiety: Therapeutic Touch and Casual Touch Groups ($N = 60$)

Source	Sum of Squares	DF	Mean Square	F
Treatments	373.55	1	373.55	9.65*
Covariate	5723.07	1	5723.07	147.90†
Error	2205.60	57	38.70	
Total	8302.22	59	6135.32	

*Significant at $p \leq 0.01$ †Significant at $p \leq 0.001$

$(1,57)$ = 9.65, $p<0.01$. After controlling for pretreatment differences in A-State anxiety, the group receiving Therapeutic Touch was found to have significantly lower scores in A-State anxiety than the Casual Touch group. Thus, hypothesis two was supported.

Subjects in the Casual Touch group functioned as a control group. Seven subjects' posttest A-State anxiety scores increased. The act of pulse-taking may have had a symbolic meaning for those subjects with cardiac pathology (Wolf, 1958; Jarvinen, 1955). Casual Touch may not have been "casual" in the usual meaning of the word. In planning the research design, the investigator wanted a procedure with which the patient would be familiar and in which there could be contact with different parts of the body. Perhaps a better term for such an intervention could have been "known touch."

Casual Touch, as described in this research, differed from the routine pulse palpation that takes place between nurse and patient in that it took much longer and was preceded by verbal information given to the patient that this increase in length of time was "part of a research procedure." Perhaps another procedure that allowed for human contact but without the personal meaning attached to "measuring the heart" may have been a more suitable control. However, 17 subjects' posttest A-State anxiety scores indicated a decrease and 6 subjects' posttest A-State anxiety scores remained the same. Examination of the posttest verbal interviews indicated such comments as, "I like to be helpful; she seemed like a nice person; it's nice to feel useful and help someone out."

It is suggested that this group functioned as intended, to measure "placebo effect." In many instances, the investigator and/or research assistant acted as a "placebo" (Frank, 1961) to stimulate feelings of helpfulness and usefulness in the subjects, and they responded in a very "useful" way, i.e., by indicating they wanted to help out on the written questionnaire.

Hypothesis Three

As indicated in Table 4, an analysis of covariance comparing the Therapeutic Touch group with the No Touch group resulted in F $(1,57)$ = 7.21, $p<0.01$. Again the group receiving Therapeutic

TABLE 4. Analysis of Covariance for A-State Anxiety: Therapeutic Touch and No Touch Groups ($N = 60$)

Source	Sum of Squares	DF	Mean Square	F
Treatments	786.96	1	786.96	7.21*
Covariate	2868.95	1	2868.95	26.29†
Error	6221.32	57	109.16	
Total	9877.23	59	3765.07	

*Significant at $p \leq 0.01$ †Significant at $p \leq 0.001$

Touch was found to have significantly lower scores on A-State anxiety than the No Touch group, supporting hypothesis three.

In some subjects receiving intervention by No Touch, there was an increase in posttest A-State anxiety. An analysis of data recorded during this intervention indicates that those patients spoke of events that were emotionally upsetting: death of spouse, fear of losing a job, family support, loneliness of hospitalization, fear of impending surgery or a clinical procedure.

Although it is often assumed that talking with patients is reassuring and comforting, there is literature that indicates that when patients talk about emotionally sensitive topics, the heart rate, blood pressure, and cardiac rhythms may be affected (Wolf and Goodell, 1976; Sigler, 1967; DiMascio, Boyd, and Greenblatt, 1957). In this research design, there was time for subjects to introduce areas of concern or worry but not enough time for resolution of any of the material. Some of the interview content would need considerable time, beyond hospitalization, for resolution. This intervention may be considered a limitation of this study, or it may document a reality factor in our hospital environment today. Busy health professionals, including nurses, with a limited amount of time for patient interaction often quickly ask patients, "How are you doing today?" or "How is it going?" This is done to show concern and to comfort the patient. However, if the patient does not have adequate time for interaction or if the material evoked is uncomfortable for him/her, the opposite physiological effect of anxiety may be produced. In short-term interactions, if a state of relaxation is primarily desirable, body therapies, including Therapeutic Touch, may help to produce this state more quickly for the patient.

Ancillary Analysis

In order to determine whether the Casual Touch group differed from the No Touch group, after adjusting for initial pretreatment differences, an additional analysis of covariance was performed for these two groups. The results indicate that the Casual Touch and No Touch groups were not significantly different (F (1,57) = 1.11, $p < 0.05$) in posttreatment A-State anxiety after taking into account pretreatment differences in A-State anxiety.

Although the sample in this study is small, there is no statistical support to indicate that the differences in pre- and posttest A-State anxiety scores in subjects receiving intervention by Therapeutic Touch were related to sex, religious background, ethnicity, reason for hospitalization, or whether the subject meditated or practiced relaxation exercises on a regular basis. Further examination of data was done to determine whether there was a relationship between a decrease in A-State anxiety and the subjects' pre-A-State anxiety score. Statistical analysis indicated no relationship between these scores.

The mean score for pre-A-State anxiety for this sample was 41.1. It is lower than the mean score reported in research where cardiovascular patients were tested on admission to the hospital (Gentry et al., 1972). This relatively low mean score may be accounted for by the fact that patients with heart disease tend to deny the feelings of anxiety they experience, and the clinical environment supports this denial by fostering a great deal of hope in the outcome of the illness (Hackett and Weisman, 1969).

Implications for Professional Nursing

Research on Therapeutic Touch documents and lends further support to nursing research and clinical practice showing the effects of interpersonal relationships on patient care. For a long time this aspect of care has been less appreciated and acknowledged for its healing functions in favor of objective scientific data. For example, early behavioral research so clearly demonstrated the power of human contact that it became important for scientific investigators to carefully "control" for its effects and "isolate" the object of study from the investigator. Before the advent of the scientific era of health care, helping persons were forced to rely on their own presence as a source of helping and/or healing. The history of health care since that time has been increasingly less mindful of the effects of the "bedside manner" or human contact, and more and more dependent on the effects of drugs and technological advances to aid recovery. Therapeutic Touch makes its unique contribution by offering a framework for understanding the potency of the human organism as a resource in healing and recovery care.

It was observed that some subjects in the No Touch group had an increase in anxiety and that their comments in the verbal posttest interview indicated worry and concern. A future area of research could be to investigate whether the patients with increased amounts of anxiety, such as in crisis states, would be able to decrease their anxiety through verbal means if Therapeutic Touch was combined with the verbal stimulation.

This study could be replicated with a different patient population and a different age group. It would also be of interest to lengthen the intervention period to two days or longer in order to observe the differences in A-State anxiety posttest scores between the first and subsequent days in each of the three groups. It is important to replicate this study with other nurses administering Therapeutic Touch intervention.

Research is needed to explore the effects of Therapeutic Touch on physiological indices of anxiety, such as pulse rate, blood pressure, and heart rate and rhythm. What is the effect of Therapeutic Touch on sleep and rest patterns of hospitalized patients? Future research could utilize patient reports, nurse observations, and/or EOG recordings to determine this relationship.

Lesh's (1970) research indicates that subjects who practice meditation improve their empathic abilities and their degree of openness to experience. The training of the mind to stay in the present moment allows reality to be experienced directly and spontaneously. Learning to perceive the world unconditionally in this manner allows a direct experience of oneself and the other. From this framework, Therapeutic Touch, as a meditative state of consciousness, could aid health professionals to grasp more intuitively their patients' concerns and experiences with greater ease and clarity.

An area of acknowledged concern for nurses and all health professionals today is how to manifest an attitude of care and concern and deliver quality health care while working actively with patients over long periods of time, and often under high stress conditions. The tedium and tiredness that may result from such intense and demanding situations has been described as the "burnout syndrome" (Shubin, 1978). Therapeutic Touch is a modality that may offer some ways to counteract such a state, for by its nature it emphasizes that the practitioner "center" and acknowledge self as the "channel" for healing energies, not become the "source" of these energies. Future research could explore whether or not the centered state, in which Therapeutic Touch is practiced, does assist the nurse to maintain an openness to the patients' experience and whether it decreases anxiety and stress related to the nurse–patient relationship.

Weiss (1979) has encouraged research that explores the meaning of touch in terms of its symbols and universal meanings. Similar questions could be asked regarding Therapeutic Touch: What are the symbols in the "language" of Therapeutic Touch? Does Therapeutic Touch have universal meanings regardless of circumstantial conditions? This could be explored through personal interview data, imagery techniques, and questionnaires regarding the healer's and healee's personal responses to the intervention of Therapeutic Touch.

Bibliography

Barnett, K. A theoretical construct of the concepts of touch as they relate to nursing. *Nursing Research*, 1972, 21, 102–110.

Benson, H., Beary, J. F. and Carol, M. P. The relaxation response. *Psychiatry*, 1974, 37, 37–46.

Burr, H.S. *Blueprint for immortality: the electric patterns of life.* London: Neville Spearman, 1972.

Cannon, W.B. The emergency function of the adrenal medulla in pain and the major emotions. *American Journal of Physiology*, 1914, 33, 356-372.

DiMascio A., Boyd, R. W. and Greenblatt, M. Physiological correlates of tension and antagonism during psychotherapy: a study of interpersonal physiology. *Psychosomatic Medicine*, 1957, *19*, 104–113.

Frank, J. *Persuasion and healing*. Baltimore: Johns Hopkins Press, 1961.

Gellhorn, E. and Keily, W.F. Mystical states of consciousness: neurophysiological and clinical aspects. *Journal of Nervous and Mental Diseases*, 1972, *154*, 8, 399–405.

Gentry, W.D., Foster, S. and Honey, T. Denial as a determinant of anxiety and health status in the coronary care unit. *Psychosomatic Medicine*, 1972, *34*, 39-44.

Hackett, T.P. and Weisman, A.D. Denial as a factor in patients with heart disease and cancer. *Annals of the New York Academy of Sciences*, 1969, *164*, 802–811.

Hartman, E. *The function of sleep*. New Haven: Yale University Press, 1973.

Jarvinen, K. Can ward rounds be a danger to patients with myocardial infarction? *British Medical Journal*, 1955, 318–320.

Krieger, D. The relationship of touch, with intent to help or to heal, to subjects' in-vivo hemoglobin values: a study in personalized interaction. *Proceedings of the ninth ANA nursing research conference*. Kansas City: American Nurses' Association, 1973.

Krieger, D. Healing by the laying-on of hands as a facilitator of bioenergetic change: the response of in-vivo human hemoglobin. *Psychoenergetics*, 1974, *1*, 121–219.

Krieger, D. Therapeutic Touch: the imprimatur of nursing. *American Journal of Nursing*, 1975, *75*, 784–787.

Krieger, D., Peper, E., and Ancoli, S. Therapeutic Touch: searching for evidence of physiological change. *American Journal of Nursing*, 1979, *4*, 660–662.

Lesh, T. U. Zen meditation and the development of empathy in counselors. *Journal of Humanistic Psychology*, 1970, *10*, 39–74.

Lynch, J., Malinow, K., Thomas, S. and Mills, M. Effects of human contact on the heart activity of curarized patients in a shock-trauma unit. *American Heart Journal*, 1974a, *88*, 169–179.

Lynch, J., Thomas, S., Mills, M., Malinow, K. and Katcher, A. The effects of human contact on cardiac arrhythmia in coronary care patients. *Journal of Nervous and Mental Diseases*, 1974b, *155*, 88–97.

McCorkle, R. Effects of touch on seriously ill patients. *Nursing Research*, 1974, *23*, 195–232.

Mills, M. E., Thomas, S. A., Lynch, J. J. and Katcher, A. H. Effect of pulse palpation on cardiac arrhythmia in coronary care patients. *Nursing Research*, 1976, *25*, 378–382.

Ravitz, L. J. Electro-magnetic field monitoring changing state functions including hypnotic states. *Journal of American Society of Psychosomatic Dentistry and Medicine*, 1970, *17*, 4.

Rogers, M. *An introduction to the theoretical basis of nursing*. Philadelphia: F. A. Davis, 1970.

Rubin, R. Maternal touch. *Nursing Outlook*, 1963, *11*, 828–831.

Shubin, S. Burnout: the professional hazards you face in nursing. *Nursing,* 1978, 78, 822–825.

Sigler, L. H. Emotion and atherosclerotic heart disease. I: electrocardiographic changes observed on the recall of past emotional disturbances. *British Journal of Medical Psychology,* 1967, 40, 55–61.

Spielberger, C. D. *Anxiety and behavior.* Vol. 1. New York: Academic Press, 1966.

Spielberger, C. D., Gorsuch, R. L., and Lushene, R. E. *STAI manual for the state-trait anxiety inventory.* Palo Alto, Calif.: Consulting Psychologists Press, Inc., 1970.

Tart, C. T. *Altered states of consciousness.* New York: Anchor Books, 1969.

Tart, C.T. *States of consciousness.* New York: E.P. Dutton, 1975.

Tiller, W.A. New fields, new laws. In White, J. and Krippner, S. (Eds.), *Future science.* New York: Anchor Books/Doubleday, 1977, pp. 28–34.

Weiss, S. J. The language of touch. *Nursing Research,* 1979, 28, 76–80.

Wolf, S. Cardiovascular reactions to symbolic stimuli. *Circulation,* 1958, 18, 287–292.

Wolf, S. and Goodell, H. *Behavioral science in clinical medicine.* Springfield, Ill.: Charles C Thomas, 1976.

PART III

Patients' Responses to Therapeutic Touch

In this section we examine the healee's participation in and responses to Therapeutic Touch. A study of healing from a holistic perspective must not only include the healee's responses but must address the issue of how the healer–healee interaction affects the healing process. Healing in Therapeutic Touch cannot be considered as something "done to" a healee but rather as a healer–healee encounter at a particular point in space and time.

This final section includes anecdotal accounts of the healee's perceptions of Therapeutic Touch. These reflect the personal nature of the experience and the uniqueness of each person's encounter. However, certain themes emerge from the material presented. These healees describe one of the main reactions to Therapeutic Touch to be the realization that they had more responsibility for their own state of health than they had allowed themselves to recognize. Some acknowledge that self-attitudes are reflected in the state of physical health. The caring relationship between healer and healee often provided the milieu in which change could occur. These first-person accounts also bring to light the fact that healing does not mean symptom removal but rather may entail facing repressed material which, while unrecognized, impeded healing.

In addition to the subjective data written by recipients of Therapeutic Touch, two articles in this section describe healees' responses through the use of questionnaires and imagery techniques. The results of these studies coincide closely with the accounts written by the patients. Taken together, the chapters in this section present some initial attempts to further our understanding of the healer–healee interchange.

Chapter 13

Healer-Healee Interactions and Beliefs in Therapeutic Touch: Some Observations and Suggestions

Rene Beck
Erik Peper

The "river of healing" is always present in the world. Like life itself, it defies definition, but is an active force manifesting at all levels of existence. It can be touched in many ways, often unexpectedly. As often as not it is passed by unseen, or unrecognized, for it is usually the conditions within the patient himself which obscure its presence and obstruct its beneficent flow.

(Theosophical Research Centre, 1958, p. 7)

The qualities that optimize the healing contact during Therapeutic Touch are of primary importance to every person learning to heal. We studied the interactions of Therapeutic Touch at a two-week training program at Pumpkin Hollow residential retreat in upstate New York, in which both patients (healees) and practitioners (healers) lived in a communal setting. By observing the extent to which the relationship between healees and healers and the patient's own beliefs affected the healing process, we hoped to obtain useful information which would help in the practice and teaching of Therapeutic Touch. We hypothesized that the efficacy of Therapeutic Touch is related to the attitudes or psychological states of the healees as well as to what extent the patients believed they could affect the outcome of their own healing process. At this training program, under the direction of Dolores Krieger and Dora Kunz, approximately 80 health professionals learned beginning and advanced Therapeutic Touch, a process akin to the laying-on of hands (Krieger, 1974; Krieger, 1979; Krieger, Peper, and Ancoli, 1979). The retreat encouraged an atmosphere of caring, support, and the development of self-healing potentials in patients and healers alike.

Each of the 13 patients (some of whom eventually became healers) received on the average nine healings, from an average of nine healers. Their illnesses ranged from lead poisoning to chronic hepatitis to progressive blindness. At the end of the two-week retreat, the healees, including the ones who had become healers (mean age 37.5, range 25 to 60 years), filled out both an objective and an open-ended questionnaire which explored the attitudes and subjective experiences related to received healing. The findings of these questionnaires serve as the basis for this chapter.

Observations from the Questionnaire

Exploring the healer–healee interaction, we found that the quality of the relationship between healee and healer appeared paramount in affecting the healing process. The workshop leaders had already emphasized their perceived importance of the relationship between healer and healee, and the healee's own attitude. Healees also perceived that their own belief systems (of which the healing relationship was a part) affected the healing. We also found that all healees reported that the healing experience was "successful" (see Figure 1). Interestingly, the efficacy of the subjective report of healing did not appear to be related to the severity of the diagnosed illness.

The patients reported that a number of their symptoms had diminished. These symptoms were both physical and emotional. One healee reported the disappearance of skin cancer, while another experienced an increase in personal strength and confidence, enabling her to "pick up her life" once again. A third patient felt that repatterning on an emotional level had taken place.

Although the healees' observations are, of course, idiosyncratic,

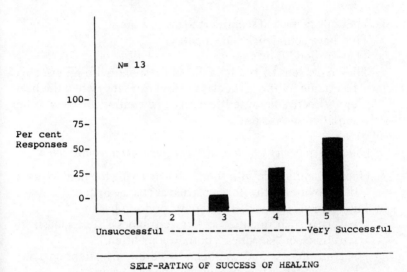

SELF-RATING OF SUCCESS OF HEALING

Figure 1. Patients' self-reported successful effect of Therapeutic Touch at the end of the healing period.

two major categories of response stand out: (1) factors affecting the relationship between the healee and the healer, and (2) factors affecting the healees' beliefs. In the following section, these two categories are presented and illustrated by healees' descriptions.

Factors Affecting the Relationship Between Healee and Healer

✳ *Qualities in healer which made healee feel comfortable.* Ten of the 13 healees reported that healers who manifest the following qualities encouraged them to feel comfortable in the relationship:

Charact. would have to include

They are secure in what they are doing or are open to learning.
They are more stable and clear, and are thus better channels.
I can relate to them as friends, and I sense in them a feeling of concern and compassion.
They are experienced.

They talk to me and seem alert to my reactions.

They have confidence and empathy.

They are gentle and strong.

They have sensitivity, the ability to respond with an effective technique for my particular needs. I can sense when the healer is effective because I feel relief or comfort or some other sensation such as heat.

Qualities in healer which made the healee feel uncomfortable

I feel uncomfortable with those who are trying too hard to prove their abilities or to effect a particular change in me.

They exhibit fogginess, uncertainty, pride, or hastiness.

They have such qualities as "powertripiness," coarseness, insensitivity, or "kookiness" or they don't listen.

Their unsureness and "wobbliness" drew my attention away from meditative thoughts during the healing process.

They seemed uncertain.

Qualities of techniques that healer used which made healee feel comfortable

They are slow, calm, and do not talk, thus breaking the meditative feeling.

They touch in quick light strokes.

They give an occasional touch so I know where their hands are. I like to know what they are doing.

Qualities of techniques that healer used which made healee feel uncomfortable

Their hands shake, especially if they are touching me; they make quick or abrupt movements.

They project anxiety.

They rely upon verbal directions.

Factors Affecting the Healee's Beliefs

Although the healing appears to be affected partly by the qualities of the healer, most healees find it difficult to give feedback to the healer because of the implicit authority–subject relationship. This absence of openness to sharing nonjudgmentally may block the healing experience. In fact, five healees reported that they had refrained from telling the healer that things he/she did made them uncomfortable. These reports indicate that healers must (1) take into account the reticence of healees to share information, and (2) actively encourage healees to share their interactional experiences.

Personality qualities in the healee which affected the healing

I am too much a "Type A" personality.

I tend to lock in feelings, have always tended to the stiff-upper-lip style. If I have a pain, illness, or stress, my tendency is to keep it internalized.

I am very sensitive and have a somewhat negative self-image; I am a high achiever.

Social/environmental qualities of the healee which affected the healing

Stress has been a problem for me for about two years. It has to do with the family.

Of course, undue stress can injure. Supportive situations are healing.

My work seems to evoke my negative self-image. I feel inadequate, don't have self-confidence.

Personal beliefs of the healee which affected the healing

Usually when I believe I'll get well, I do.

Keeping an open mind and seeing myself as capable of growth and development helps me to be healthy.

I believe that illness as a crisis can be turned into a learning and growth experience. My belief in God also influences the healing process.

Observations

The patients' beliefs and experiences may affect the healing process. The data indicate that a nonjudgmental, relaxed attitude reduces illness onset and may possibly encourage self-healing. These attitudes should be encouraged in the healee.

This study is not the first to reveal that patients have certain preferences about the type of qualities in and techniques used by their healers. For example, while there are many patients who prefer to be touched, there are some who do not. Similarly, some patients report that meditating or visualizing during the healing helps them become receptive to the healing while others prefer to sit quietly. As Ilkin (1958) states:

> The great thing in all spiritual healing is the arousing of faith of the patient to the point at which healing forces, physical and mental, can dominate the organism. . . . This may need different methods for each patient. Each can acquire it in his own way [p. 8].

Essentially, healers have to become aware of the uniqueness of each healee, since healees most likely will not reveal any discomfort about the process. Healers who are confident, certain, stable, sensitive, gentle, and compassionate must encourage communication from the healee. Our observations of the importance of a trusting and intimate healee-healer relationship confirm the Theosophical Research Centre (1958) observation of the doctor-patient interaction:

> Thus psychological conditioning in the patient, and certain factors in the physician which can only be called psychic or spiritual, combine to make the doctor–patient relationship both intricate and intimate [p. 15].

The healing process often mobilizes the healees' self-healing potential. To allow the self-healing to continue, the healees need to reassess, reevaluate, and change their illness-producing life-styles, relationships, and thinking patterns. Healees in this study revealed a heightened awareness of the way they contributed to their own disease processes, such as through negative self-images, destructive interpersonal relationships, or undesirable working conditions. This recognition is the first step toward becoming responsible for one's own health. Such self-awareness is an important factor for the high rate of reported successes and positive outcomes. As one patient remarked, "Usually when I believe I'll get well, I do."

The supportive, caring, relaxed atmosphere in which the subjects of this study lived for a two-week period must be counted as a major factor in the high rate of patient improvement. Thus, it seems difficult to draw a line between the degree of influence of the unique environment, the abilities of the healers, the relationship between patient and healer, and the individual healee him/herself. It is most reasonable to assume that an interaction of all these factors combines to create the effective healing.

The healer may learn to optimize the interactive healing process by including and accounting for the following five concepts in the approach to healing:

What we communicate by word, act, and attitude, and our setting, will affect our potential for change. Everything, from our choice of words to the type of room in which we practice, communicates something. There is no way to avoid communicating. Silence is an important message. When a friend passes without looking at us or speaking to us, we assume he is angry with us. When a doctor avoids answering a question about our health, we assume the worst (Peper and Kushel, 1979).

What we believe is important. Of the many things we communicate, the most essential is our belief. What we believe affects our self-image. It affects our actions. It affects our health and our capacity for self-healing. For example, in a recent UCLA study, Schweiger and Parducci (1978) reported that two-thirds of the subjects studied reported mild headaches when they were told that the experiment, which involved passing an electrical current through their heads, might cause a headache. In fact, no electricity was used.

Again and again we observed that if the practitioner believed that the participant could change the temperature of his hand and conveyed that by choice of words, tone, and attitude, the participant was much more likely to succeed than if any negativity was present. Further, when someone does, for instance, raise his own hand temperature and biofeedback equipment tells him so, his belief in his ability to change is heightened (Peper and Kushel, 1979).

Every part is connected to every other part, and every part in the system affects every other part. We are all part of the system—the participant, his family, the healer. They are all interconnected in a network and have an effect on each other. There is no such thing as an independent observer. The moment one observes, the system is affected. Here our premises match those of physics—when one observes a particle, one affects it (Peper and Kushel, 1979).

Qualities which are critical may be too subtle to measure or observe. Even something that is not measured can affect the results. The observation that traditional electromagnetic measures do not measure auras does not imply that auras do not exist, only that the equipment does not measure them. Only once in a while can we prove the nonexistence of a phenomenon.

Time may expand or contract. The effect of healing may not occur at the time period immediately following the healing. Preliminary observation suggests that maximum effect may be observed four hours after the healing.

To explore and apply Therapeutic Touch, healers must account for the previous five concepts, even though strict scientific analysis may impede the healing potential. Healing processes may be observed and measured by (1) the change in attitude and clinical outcome in the healee, and (2) the change in the healer's approach to the healing interaction. If healing efficacy improves, this implies that this (changed) variable is an important aspect in the healing process.

Conclusion

This study observed that the healees' view of the healee-healer interaction is an important factor in the healing process. From the responses of the healees, we can now emphasize from a more scientific and systematic point of view that the attitude of the patient toward the healer, and therefore toward the healing relationship, plus the attitude of the patient about him/herself and the way he/she relates to the environment are decisive factors in a more effective "cure." We suggest that any study which teaches, practices, or investigates healing needs to address the issues raised by the five previously described concepts which affect the healing process.

Bibliography

Ilkin, P. *Mystery of healing*. Wheaton, Ill.: Theosophical Publishing House, 1958.

Krieger, D. Healing by the laying-on of hands as a facilitator of bioenergetic change: the response of in-vivo human hemoglobin. *International Journal of Psychoenergetic Systems*, 1974, *1*, 121–129.

Krieger, D. *The Therapeutic Touch: how to use your hands to help or to heal*. Englewood Cliffs, N.J.: Prentice-Hall, 1979.

Krieger, D., Peper, E. and Ancoli, S. Therapeutic Touch: searching for evidence of physiological change. *American Journal of Nursing*, 1979, *79*, 660–662.

Peper, E. and Kushel, C. An holistic merger of biofeedback and family therapy. *American Theosophist*, 1979, *67*, 158–168.

Schweiger, A. and Parducci, A. Placebo in reverse. *Brain-Mind Bulletin*, 1978, *3*, 1.

Theosophical Research Centre. *The mystery of healing*. Wheaton, Ill.: Theosophical Publishing House, 1958.

Chapter 14
My Introduction to Therapeutic Touch

Iris Wolfson

I have long had an active involvement in the healing arts, both in my professional and in my personal life. My education in nursing was in a traditional nursing program which placed the emphasis on the care of the physcial body, using the scientific approach. It soon became apparent to me that disease has causes and dimensions far beyond the purely physical and that it did not make sense to invalidate other approaches to health care simply because they could not be explained in scientific terms. My growing awareness of limitations inherent in the allopathic approach to health care evolved into an exploration of various alternative health practices. In searching for a better understanding of holistic concepts, I came upon an article about Therapeutic Touch which sparked my curiosity.

I registered as a participant in a healers' workshop that was to focus on Therapeutic Touch. When I applied to the workshop my intention was to learn the practice and theory of Therapeutic Touch from the healer's perspective. To my surprise, however, most of my learning during this period was a result of my experiences as a recipient of Therapeutic Touch intervention.

It wasn't until after I arrived at the workshop that I considered asking to be the subject in a healing session, but there were two areas of concern that I hoped might be helped by Therapeutic Touch. The first was the result of a traumatic automobile accident that had occurred six weeks before the workshop. Emergency abdominal surgery had been required, and I was hoping that Therapeutic Touch could accelerate my recuperation. The second and greater concern was a chronic pelvic inflammatory condition.

The pelvic inflammatory disease was a result of an intrauterine device that had been in place for two-and-a-half years. The initial inflammatory process had begun about two years prior to my attendance at the healers' workshop. At that time I had experienced six months of a recurrent, acute pelvic inflammation which was accompanied by moderate to severe pain, requiring complete bed rest on numerous occasions. After antibiotic, then herbal, naturopathic, and nutritional treatments failed, I eventually sought homeopathic therapy. After about a month of this treatment the severe and frequent recurrences started to subside. During the next year and a half I experienced mild and occasional moderate exacerbations of the inflammation at two- to three-month intervals, despite my continuing homeopathic therapy. There was always a reminder that all was not well.

When I volunteered as a healee, my primary interest was in obtaining help for this pelvic inflammatory disease, as I felt that I was healing well from the abdominal surgery. I was fortunate to receive Therapeutic Touch daily for about three days, and then on five or six more occasions during the ten-day period.

As a recipient of Therapeutic Touch, my first awareness was of a profound relaxation. I began to experience a sense of tranquility and inner unity which deepened as the Therapeutic Touch continued. On occasion I was aware of a feeling of warmth or tingling around and within my body. My perceptions during Therapeutic Touch seemed to be more connected with internal feelings than with physical sensations. I often felt very close to the healers and experienced a different level of understanding and intimacy with another person than I had known before. I was aware of a very definite relationship being shared by myself and the healers. A tremendous sensation of acceptance, compassion, and love was evident. For the first time I began to develop a conscious awareness of the flow of energy within and surrounding us all, and I felt very open and receptive to the subtle energy exchanges between myself and the healers. This recognition of and receptivity to the energy flow extended to a sense of awareness and connection to the flow of energy among all living things. A heightened state of awareness was developing, and with it came a pervasive feeling of peace and well-being.

This open and receptive state, however, included an aspect of vulnerability that occasionally caused me to experience some very intense emotional episodes. These related both to the pelvic inflammatory process and to the automobile accident. I later came to understand that this vulnerability permitted an emotional release which was an integral part of the healing process for me. This was a vital component of the healing experience which I had not considered or appreciated at first.

After several of my initial Therapeutic Touch encounters I became very tearful and upset. Many repressed thoughts and feelings resulting from the trauma of the accident and surgery began to surface to conscious awareness. I now had access to some previously blocked emotional content that I was able to confront, deal with, and then let go. The open state that Therapeutic Touch produced in me resulted in its reaching and affecting me on many levels. It forced me to focus on some very painful and unresolved emotional aspects of my condition. I realized later that a primary factor in my healing was the psychological integration of the traumatic episodes. The physical healing was only one aspect of the healing process, and I needed to work through the emotional blocks before healing could be complete. I was surprised to learn how deeply and on how many levels Therapeutic Touch was able to contact me.

Also reaching me on an emotional level was a concern relating to the pelvic inflammatory disease. During one of the Therapeutic Touch sessions there was a discussion about the impact that pelvic inflammatory disease can have on one's sexuality, and the guilt and anxieties that are produced regarding one's childbearing capabilities. These comments were made after the Therapeutic Touch assessment had been completed. This discussion seemed to introduce some negativity into the healing session, and almost immediately I became extremely upset and tearful. I was filled with fears about whether I could ever become pregnant. While it was important for me to reexamine and confront these anxieties, it also became clear to me that the healee is in an extremely vulnerable state during a healing and is particularly sensitive to outside influences, both positive and negative.

Later in the workshop, I was taught about the use of positive imagery, and how images can directly relate to the body's energy patterns. Through my experience as a healee I came to understand more fully the importance of being careful about the imagery that language can produce; I am now acutely aware of this when I am in the healer role. I am always very careful to present a positive outlook and not to imprint negative images.

As the workshop progressed there were times when I did not feel open and receptive to energy exchange. I began to feel increasingly more frustrated with being in the healee role. I was anxious to help and not to be helped, to get out of the healee and into the healer role. I wanted to give and was finding it more and more difficult to accept. My frustration overwhelmed and blocked me from receiving the full benefit of the later Therapeutic Touch healings. It was hard for me at the time to realize how much I was learning from my experiences as a healee and of the need to be healthy oneself before practicing as an effective healer.

It has been nine months since my first encounter with Therapeutic Touch. I have had only one mild episode of pelvic inflammatory disease during this time and believe that the therapeutic effects that originated during the workshop are continually deepening. I feel that I am able to work within myself to continue my healing, and I am approaching my fear about pregnancy in a more constructive way. My abdominal incision has healed well, and I have been able to release much of the trauma from the accident, allowing me to drive without fear. I am enjoying a continuing sensation of opening up to new ways of perceiving the world, an extension of the expansive feeling I encountered throughout the workshop. Previously, my understanding of holistic health was on an intellectual level. Now, in addition, this experiential aspect is an invaluable part of my personal and professional growth.

The experience of being a healee has also enhanced my ability to integrate the theoretical knowlege with the practical application of Therapeutic Touch. I have been using Therapeutic Touch as a healing modality in a variety of circumstances during these past months, and I am continually inspired by the feedback I receive. During one of my first Therapeutic Touch attempts, I was especially touched by the response of a woman in labor. I was gently stroking and smoothing the energy field above her abdomen, but she did not know that I was practicing Therapeutic Touch. Her previous agitated state softened, and she afterwards asked what I had been doing. She described to me her overwhelming feeling of relaxation and well-being and of an awareness on her part of her baby also experiencing this relaxation. Her emotional state became much more mellow, her tension was alleviated, and she was able to progress from a slow labor pattern to a more active one. She proceeded after several hours to give joyous birth to an eight-pound boy!

Editors' note: The author, in a note sent to the editors soon after completion of the manuscript for this chapter, said she was three months pregnant!

Chapter 15

A Skeptic's Response to Therapeutic Touch

Philip Caleb

I am a 46-year-old male who until 1969 had an unremarkable medical history. At that time I was an officer in the USAF stationed in Vietnam and subject to an intense flying schedule. After several months I became aware of a decrease in night vision and also experienced occasional periods of double vision. I assumed these visual problems were due to stress and fatigue. I was flying up to ten hours a night, and on flights that long and under those conditions, eye strain is to be expected. When I returned to the United States, the double vision seemed to disappear, but I did notice that my reading speed had slowed considerably. I occasionally wore reading glasses and decided to have my prescription updated. The flight surgeon took one look at my eyes and referred me to an ophthalmologist. He discovered I had persistent double vision and had over 50 percent decrease in night vision. For all practical purposes I was blind in the right eye. He diagnosed my condition as being an atypical case of retinitis pigmentosa, and I was hospitalized for further evaluation.

For the first six months of 1970 I was in and out of half-a-dozen military and civilian hospitals and clinics. At the time it seemed as if I was being given every test then known to medical science. My left eye was normal, except for a reduced peripheral field. Only minimal peripheral vision remained in the right eye, and I had limited extraocular movement in all directions. Lumbar punctures showed elevated cerebrospinal-fluid protein, and my body balance was affected. EKGs were normal, and no muscle weakness was noted at that time. Physically, I felt reasonably well. However, the lack of a diagnosis and a prognosis left me with considerable mental and psychological stress. In retrospect, it was more than I could realize at the time.

By the autumn of 1970 I had been placed on the inactive list by the Air Force and had retired to a rural area of northern Vermont. The Air Force continued a medical evaluation of my condition every 18 months, and for the next four years little change was observed in my physical condition. However, I became progressively isolated socially and psychologically and unable to deal with the anger and hostility within me. I slowly alienated myself from everyone and everything. Although there were other factors involved, this alienation, induced in part by my physical condition, was the most significant reason for the breakup of my marriage in 1975.

I moved to a small city where my wife had relocated, hoping to reestablish my marriage through counseling, but was unable to open up enough to receive any benefit from these therapies. By late 1975 my drinking had increased to the point where I had to have a drink before I could get out of bed in the morning. At this point, a kind of quantum leap transpired, sparked by a dream, and I became conscious of life again. Suddenly, I realized that if I was going to survive, and evolve and grow as a whole human being, I had to initiate a change. I started therapy again, this time with more success.

In 1975–76 the Department of Neurology at the University of Vermont Medical Center determined the probable primary cause of my condition. Several small scotoma had developed in my left eye, and a partial right bundle branch block had progressed to a bifascicular block. I had poor body coordination, muscle weakness, and a loss of strength, especially in the upper extremities. Muscle biopsies indicated that the mitochondria in the muscle cells were not doing their job and were at the root of the problem. At long last it was a relief to have a diagnosis. Because of the rarity of this condition, no prognosis was given to me. Moreover, I did not have any idea as to what might have caused the disease to develop in the first place. I became more social, but the anger and hostility that remained within me continued to stymie my openness and growth.

The wall of blind trust I have always had toward traditional medicine was cracked in 1970 during my first hospitalization. I was faced with the decision of whether or not to give the doctor permission to do some additional painful tests. I felt they would not make any difference to my condition, and plaintively voiced these feelings to a priest who visited me. He told me, "You are responsible for your body; trust your feelings." That comment threw me since I expected from him reinforcement of medical authority. I decided later to have the tests done. I have related this to make the point that in order for Therapeutic Touch to be effective one must possess, as a precondition, an awareness that the care of the body is a personal responsibility. One must also have some degree of sensitivity to the body's signals and messages.

A nurse told me about a Healing Workshop at Pumpkin Hollow Farm in New York. This was the summer of 1977. At this time I felt neutral to adjunctive kinds of healing, and since I trusted her I decided it was worth a try. This brings up the second condition I think necessary for Therapeutic Touch to be effective. The patient must trust, or at least be open to, the healing interaction. Doubts and skepticism are not limitations so long as one can be open and objectively critical of the consideration that there may be other means than traditional medicine to accomplish healing.

Prior to the ten-day workshop I had practically no eye movement on a horizontal plane, no elevation upward on a vertical plane, but some control of downward movement. By the end of the healing workshop I had recovered 20 to 25 percent of normal lateral movement, sufficient to resume driving on a limited basis. During the treatments, I occasionally felt apprehensive, but there were no side effects. I would feel a "tingling sensation" as the healer's hands passed across my body. Sometimes I would also feel or "sense" warmth emanating from the healer's hands. I do not clearly remember my thought processes during healing, but usually I would try to maintain an open or meditative state. My intuition told me this would be the best way to facilitate the healing interaction. Immediately after a healing session, I would often feel very tired, and this condition lasted about an hour. This was not a draining or stress-producing feeling, but one of almost total relaxation in which all my systems were "switched off."

By the end of a second ten-day Therapeutic Touch workshop at Pumpkin Hollow in the summer of 1978, I had recovered about one-third of normal upward gaze. Therapeutic Touch had immediate, positive, healing effects on my eyes, and there has been no exacerbation since my first treatment two years ago. It is difficult to assess how Therapeutic Touch affected my muscle disease. I do know that for the last two years my condition has remained stable. I have check-ups every three months. Since beginning Therapeutic Touch, there have been only insignificant EKG changes, and my body feels stronger in general. My mental health is also changing. Therapeutic

Touch has facilitated my own innate ability to heal and care for myself.

The question of self-caring is the third point that is vital to the process of Therapeutic Touch. The nature of this intervention implies to me that there is an empathic link between patient and healer. My objective and rational self told me that feelings had nothing to do with healing. I found that caring for myself, or self-healing, was increased by learning to be "open" to the feelings of love and compassion I received from the healers. Maybe this has something to do with expectations on the part of the patient. I know that initially I had no specific expectations when I went to Pumpkin Hollow. I looked forward to a relaxed week in the mountains and not much else. I was truly astounded when healing did occur. When I became aware of the knowledge that I might be able to heal myself I was quite frightened.

I can only surmise what happened during Therapeutic Touch. There is a universal link between all life, a universal energy field. I sense that the healer channels this energy into the healee's body, and this triggers and nourishes the healee's internal capabilities to heal, causing negative energy to flow outward. I do not view the process as being spiritual in the traditional theological sense, and I am reluctant to use such terms as "mystic" or "psychic" in describing the process. I see it as quite a logical process, "rationally irrational." I believe the capability to heal is inherent in all of us, though apparently it is more evolved in some persons than in others.

Since Therapeutic Touch is by nature holistic, there cannot be a specific time frame for any one disorder to be cured. It allows for the uniqueness of each individual. If the whole universe, as an energy field, is involved in the healing process, then our traditional concepts of time and space may not apply. Moreover, it is far more important that the healer and healee be in harmony with this universal energy flow than to be overly concerned with measuring the results.

I experienced no permanent negative reactions from the healing sessions at Pumpkin Hollow, but I recall two particular instances of discomfort. Healing was usually conducted within a group composed of a dozen or more healers and healees. During my first participation I apparently picked up the negative energy being channeled out of the other healees. The sensation was similar to that which one has when acutely embarrassed. It was a hot, flushed, tingling sensation, debilitating and deenergizing. Once I realized what was happening it was no longer a problem. I don't know how I became aware of what was transpiring—it just happened.

The other incident occurred during my second year at Pumpkin Hollow. A physician visiting the workshop was practicing an assessment of me. He was extremely skilled at internal visualization. As he passed his hands over my body and "sensed" areas of internal imbalance, he began to imagine these diseased areas. I began to feel pain in these areas. I asked him to stop and another healer quickly "balanced" me, and the tension left. Obviously, there is more to healing than being able to visualize.

Initially it seemed very important to me that my healers know all the clinical details of my physical condition prior to healing. Gradually I began to realize that every aspect of my existence was interrelated and that the physical disorder was only one part of me that needed healing. I began to perceive my healing in holistic terms and realized that if my healers were interested only in physical details they would be healing only a part of me. Therapeutic Touch, however, involves more than visualizing the areas of disease. It involves healing the whole person.

It seems to me very important for the healer to be able to be a channel for genuine concern and affection. This is not necessarily on a verbal level. Therapeutic Touch often takes place in a quiet, relaxed, peaceful situation with a minimum of vocalization. Both of my healing experiences happened in a matter of minutes, or so it seemed to me. Actually, I now realize that an educational process had been going on for some time that had allowed and prepared me to be open to the affection and compassion I experienced in these moments of healing.

I am presently involved with several healing groups in my own area. I plan to return to Pumpkin Hollow, and this time I will be a student as well as a patient. I practice meditation and imagery on a regular basis and have had signficant results with imagery. In the last three months lateral eye movement has increased another 10 to 15 degrees. My extraocular muscles are about two-thirds the normal size. I also have found imagery and color visualization not only effective in coping with emotional and psychological stress but superior to aspirin in alleviating the pain and discomfort associated with headaches and colds.

Chapter 16

Therapeutic Touch for a Toxic State

Christina Lukasiewicz

Therapeutic Touch opened up a whole new perspective on health for me when I began that mode of treatment just over a year ago. I requested Therapeutic Touch at that time because I was greatly incapacitated by a then undiagnosed lead poisoning and malabsorption syndrome. My symptoms consisted of extreme fatigue, allergic reactions, intolerance to many foods, constant hunger, considerable weight loss, a variety of disturbances of the gastrointestinal tract, and a kind of mental numbing in which my concentration and organized thinking were greatly curtailed. I felt frustrated and crushed because my ability to function in my accustomed manner was largely thwarted and medical care had so far provided me with no answers.

During the past year, with Therapeutic Touch as a vital part of my treatment process, I have become healthier. I received Therapeutic Touch along with other patients in a group that met every other week. The sessions began with meditation. The healers, working in pairs, passed their hands over the surface of my body in order to identify areas of ill health. They could do this by becoming aware of changes in the sensations of their hands. The healers were amazingly accurate in this assessment process.

During the treatment phase, the healers would direct energy to me by placing their hands on or near the areas of illness. During the healing I often felt sensations of heat or coolness where this energy was being directed. I frequently experienced a beautiful sense of comfort. During the healing session I generally tried to think about being well or about healing energy flowing through me. I usually felt improved after Therapeutic Touch, although the kind and amount of improvement varied from time to time. The sessions ended with meditation and a discussion of what we had all experienced during the healing process.

I had the good fortune to meet Dora Kunz, whose observations and instructions were most helpful to me. I learned from her that I was full of toxins and poisons but that my condition was not serious. This was reassuring to me because I often felt so ill I thought I would not live. She also gave me directives for self-healing by putting healing energy through myself and told me to exercise, to practice deep breathing, and to drink plenty of fluids. When I later read medical journals I realized this advice was very appropriate for someone with my condition. Dora also perceived my defeatist attitude toward myself and my illness and she told me to work on overcoming it. These directives were reiterated by other healers. They took the initiative from time to time to give me specific suggestions on helping myself to get well. Thus, the healers incorporated concepts of wholeness and total health into their practice of Therapeutic Touch. They encouraged patients to use many healthful resources and they wanted patients to be under medical care.

My own program of health care was comprehensive. It included medical intervention with several necessary drugs, nutritious foods and nutritional supplements, acupuncture and diathermy to stimulate healing. In addition, my self-help endeavors were comprised of extensive reading of relevant literature, walking and swimming exercises, meditation, prayer, self-healing, yoga deep breathing, the use of mental imagery, and attempts to modify my attitude through self-healing.

I used self-healing twice a day. At times when I felt particularly fatigued or discouraged, I took time out to meditate and then to concentrate on healing energy flowing through me. My ability to keep a focused concentration varied from time to time and so did the benefits. Whenever concentration came more easily I became very relaxed and I experienced a sense of comfort which permeated my being. This extension of Therapeutic Touch provided me with a way of self-improvement for it always produced some desirable results, however small. My symptoms decreased, I became more energetic, and I felt more optimistic about regaining my health.

Perhaps the most difficult aspect of trying to get well was the effort to muster up a positive attitude. It was all too easy to fall into downheartedness or to indulge in self-pity. To think positively required that I stop the ever-rising doubts and self-disapproval and that I change my idea that wellness was a goal for the future. To think of myself as well in the present seemed self-deceptive when I was really feeling wretched. Yet that imagining myself as well had an incredibly uplifting effect. It brought a sense of strength, and I became more inclined to persevere in carrying on the work of becoming well. It was a struggle to start such positive thinking, and it often had to be preceded by a pep talk to myself.

It is not possible to determine specifically how Therapeutic Touch helped me to get well because many kinds of treatment were being used concurrently. However, there was no question in my mind about some of the immediate benefits I received following Therapeutic Touch. I always felt healing was taking place in me during the process. For the most part I experienced an easing of symptoms, an increase in energy and alertness, and a feeling of relaxation afterward. The improvements generally lasted several hours to several days.

An example that illustrates the facilitation of well-being in me by Therapeutic Touch and the possibility that very specific touch may be necessary for different individuals occurred on several occasions. I often developed a peculiar but very distressing nausea that sat high up in my chest near my neck. Dora used pressure around the neck as well as firm slapping strokes on my back and upper chest, which afforded me great relief from the nausea. Although other healers picked up this area of symptoms in their assessment of me, their use of brisk outward motions at my back and chest or their use of massage did not bring much alleviation of the discomfort. I found myself requesting the slapping technique. Most healers seemed reluctant to use this rather severe form of Therapeutic Touch until they realized how grateful I was for the relief it gave me.

Another example of the striking effectiveness of Therapeutic Touch occurred during a concentrated period of this treatment when I attended a 12-day workshop as a patient. I received Therapeutic Touch every day and my symptoms diminished greatly. I was able to tolerate all foods and I gained weight. This rapid and substantial improvement lasted over two months before some of the original symptoms returned.

In the Therapeutic Touch there were many therapeutic ingredients occurring all at the same time. For example, the healers became a sustaining system to me. I felt accepted by them and I felt their interest and desire to help me. The supportiveness of the group process in the healing sessions was abundantly evident. Patients and healers experienced a feeling of oneness and closeness as we meditated together, and we encouraged one another as we shared our experiences. The quiet and peacefulness of our group meetings was also conducive to therapeutic outcomes. After I saw results from Therapeutic Touch intervention, I believed it could help me. This was undoubtedly an important aspect of my healing. The skeptics may point out that it was suggestibility rather than Therapeutic Touch that brought about the benefits I experienced. To them I would have to ask, "What part have similar factors played in all the other kinds of health care I received?"

As a nurse I have used Therapeutic Touch to channel healing energy to some of my private duty patients. It was with pleasure that I heard them report specific improvements following Therapeutic Touch.

For the future I have committed myself to continued learning about Therapeutic Touch and the use of healing energy as a readily available resource for the alleviation of suffering and restoration of health.

Chapter 17

Therapeutic Touch: A Personal Experience

Mary Jean Gallagher

About two-and-a-half years ago, in January, 1977, at the age of 38, I learned that I had metastatic malignant lymphoma, a type of systemic cancer. The diagnosis followed quickly upon my discovery of a small lump on the left side of my neck and an immediate admission to St. Luke's Hospital in New York City for a week of diagnostic tests and a biopsy.

On an emotional level, the knowledge that the lump was cancerous brought profound shock. I was overwhelmed with feelings of helplessness, followed by anger and self-pity. I was obsessive about asking myself how this could have happened to me just when my life was working and my feelings about myself were the best they had ever been. I went through a period of stunned passivity.

On a concrete level, the diagnosis was equally hard to accept. I had never been really ill in my life except for the usual childhood diseases. There was no history of cancer, or indeed of any life-threatening chronic illness, in my family. My grandparents had lived long and useful lives. My only adult health problems had been that I was overweight and hypoglycemic. My hypoglycemia was under control with a medically supervised megavitamin program.

In all, I spent two weeks in the hospital undergoing tests and beginning specific treatment. The enforced passivity created an atmosphere in which I was able to relax and do some hard thinking about how I would cope with this illness. I made a decision early on that I would become actively involved in my treatment plan; it was this decision which ultimately led me to Therapeutic Touch.

I began to implement my decision to participate by buttonholing my surgeon, my oncologist, and my radiologist and asking for details about their recommended treatment: cobalt radiation followed by six months of intravenous chemotherapy with cytoxin and vincristin, plus oral prednisone. After much discussion, I chose to undergo radiation and chemotherapy because of the nature and stage of the cancer. I simultaneously consulted a homeopath, who advised me on a diet which, based on his experience with cancer patients, would assist my body in coping with the added strain to be placed on it by the radiation and chemotherapy.

I also increased my vitamin intake dramatically and checked the new dosages with the doctor who had treated me for hypoglycemia to see that they would not interfere with the chemotherapy. I researched laetrile and traveled to Pennsylvania to consult with a doctor who prescribed it. Ultimately, I decided not to attempt it, because of my fear that the laetrile dosages would force precipitate drops in my already low blood pressure.

I consulted a psychotherapist in an effort to handle the emotional upheaval resulting from the news of the cancer and was able to discontinue after six months. The therapeutic help was important, however, because I decided not to inform my mother of the cancer and I lacked a close family who would be supportive of me.

In sum, the radiation and chemotherapy, combined with my own efforts in diet and vitamins, resulted in success. I finished the treatment program in October, 1977, and have since discontinued a small dosage of chlorambucil daily. I have been completely off all drugs for eight months and my blood count is in the normal range. All traces of the disease have been absent for about two years.

With my pleasure at that outcome, it was easier to accept the devastating side effects of the orthodox medical treatment. I lost 40 pounds (not an unwelcome result), survived long bouts of nausea (I never did get around to trying marijuana, which is a specific for this), and retained my hair. I used vitamin therapy to combat individual side effects: B vitamins for cracked and bleeding lips, vitamin C to prevent ulcers, which can occur with large doses of prednisone, and vitamin E to assist with radiation burns.

I became involved with Therapeutic Touch in January, 1978, after I had completed the radiation and chemotherapy programs. My introduction came from the same homeopath who had earlier advised me on diet and cancer and who had now begun to treat me homeopathically.

I am convinced that without the radiation and chemotherapy, I would probably not be alive today. But I am also painfully aware of the limitations of medicine, which treats symptomatically rather than preventively.

I was groping for some recognition of my own feelings that we are the final authors of our own destruction or happiness and that we have within us a basic drive toward health. With this in mind, I began to seek out treatment modalities that start with this basic approach. Therapeutic Touch became one of those modalities for me.

Prior to my first intervention with Therapeutic Touch, a nurse took my treatment history and asked me what I wished to accomplish. Having just finished chemotherapy, my immediate aim was to assist my body to repair the damage done by the chemotherapy. I was underweight, severly anemic, and physically very weak; and my blood counts were low.

Therapeutic Touch intervention was done in the format of group meetings. Healers and healees all sat together in a circle with eyes closed for a meditation perod of about 40 minutes. Occasionally, directions were suggested during the meditative period to further the relaxed state and to tap that part of the human psyche capable of healing. Often during those meditations, I could sense, rather than feel, tension leaving my body and a sense of peace and happiness growing within me. Sometimes there were surges of warmth in my chest.

At the end of the period of guided relaxation, individual patients sat in chairs in the center of the circle and were assessed by two healers. During the assessment one stood in front and one in back of the patient and they passed their hands over the patient's body to pick up changes in sensory cues. After this, the treatment would begin and the healers would become a channel for energies to be directed to the area(s) of the patient's body that needed healing.

Since my situation involved a system-wide condition, the approach taken was to reinforce liver and spleen, organs affected by the disease and also necessary in the reparative efforts. For a year of biweekly meetings, healers concentrated on channeling yellow energy in a course from my liver to spleen, followed by blue energy to groin and armpits, sites of large concentrations of lymph nodes. In this case, visualizing yellow was a way of moderating the amount of energy that was channeled into a part of my body. Visualizing blue assisted the healers to intensify the healing energies to the particular part of the body that was in need. My cooperation consisted in maintaining my relaxed state and visualizing colors in concert with the healers.

I invariably felt strong surges of warmth in my torso, at times during the healing, but usually a few minutes after it ended. Sometimes, the warmth seemed to proceed along with the hands of a particular healer as they moved over my body. I could never anticipate what would occur in advance.

At all times the emphasis was holistic; the focus was not on the disease or condition per se but on the body–mind continuum and its powers to correct its own "dis-ease." We were encouraged to assume responsibility for our physical and mental states and to place our energies in a positive healing mode rather than to concentrate on symptoms causing discomfort. The role of the mind in illness or health was reinforced.

I was exhilarated by this approach. It was a mirror image of my prior approach to life. This modality concentrates on the positive and intuitive; it complements the problem-solving mode of today's scientific establishment. It is a radical turnabout from the accepted norm and, in many ways, returns autonomy to the individual.

At the end of one year of Therapeutic Touch, during which I also pursued my homeopathic treatments, my anemia was gone, my blood count normal, and I had, alas, gained back all of the weight I had lost, and some additional pounds for good measure.

In the light of these results, my treatment plan for receiving Therapeutic Touch has now been altered. My liver is still the focus as the largest gland and the organ responsible for detoxifying the body. Now, however, my adrenals are also being treated in an effort to cope with a stressful life-style, but it is too soon to evaluate results.

Since I have explored so many avenues in the health field in the past few years and since all of them proved in some way beneficial, it is difficult to assess accurately the concrete results of Therapeutic Touch. I do know that my attitude has changed to a more positive one and that the benefits I have received, though intangible, are real. And the bottom line remains the same—no trace of cancer for over two years.

Chapter 18

The Sign above the Bed Read "Please Touch Me": A Personal Account

Marsha Jane Nagelberg-Gerhard

My development as a healer has been an ongoing process. As a beginner, I was conscious only of being able to "feel" physical signs and symptoms such as severe pain or an inflammatory process during the assessment phase. I could intuit emotional distress at times, but needed to work with a more experienced healer as a partner in order to intensify my early perceptions. As the years progressed, my skills and knowledge base expanded, along with my understanding of the healing process. Today, about five years later, I can look back and smile at my growth. Coinciding with my studies as a healer under Dora Kunz and Dolores Krieger, there have been a lot of "life experiences." I've married, moved six times, helped one of my grandmothers to die, completed a master's degree, and done Ph.D. course work. When I look back as a participant-observer, I realize that much of my growth as a healer comes from needing and getting help at very critical space–times along the way.

Many of my circle of friends are also nurse-healers and they've all been most generous with their friendship and their time. Today, as I integrate a healing life-style into my daily life, I can thank each of them for their help and their support and their love.

Although my insights as a nurse-healer deepen, sharing my own experiences allows me to gain the confidence and understanding I need to continue down the path of healing and learning. This is my underlying motivation for writing this chapter in a personal style.

155

The experience I would like to share occurred about three years after my initial contact with Therapeutic Touch. The healers were two close friends and classmates, both nurses, one who had never before done Therapeutic Touch, though a very fast learner; the other, a nurse-healer for some time.

These healings first took place as I lay on a narrow stretcher in a New York City teaching hospital for over five long, long, hours, running high fevers, in great pain, and, obviously, critically ill, and then, during the following days as I "slowly" recovered from a severe systemic infection.

Stop, Look, and Listen: Tuning into My Body's Messages

I played squash that morning, as I did every Thursday morning. I liked the game. I liked the power, and I was slowly developing better playing strategies. I don't mind falling or banging into walls, sometimes. Unfortunately or fortunately, depending on how you view it, that particular morning I took a really hard fall—only this time it *really* hurt. My body suddenly seemed alive with pain.

There was a sharp and radiant throb in my lower abdomen. My whole body seemed to be resonating with angry pain and just as suddenly it subsided. I carefully got up from the floor, and although I felt shaken and looked pale, my squash partner and I joked about the "hard knocks of life." After catching my breath, I picked up my racquet and we finished the session. I lost the game.

As I walked off the court, a sinking feeling crept into me. The pain had come back as a gentle reminder that something was clearly wrong, but I chose not to attend to the matter just then. Other things to do and places to go. Within several hours it became quite clear that the only place I was going to was straight to the hospital. I did not pass "go," I did not "collect $200"; I went "directly to jail"— the hospital bed.

Still thinking logically, and feeling too weak to do it alone, I brought along a friend who, as a nurse, could be my advocate, my spokesperson, my protector, and, ultimately, though she'd never done Therapeutic Touch before, my healer.

Several medical examinations later, it was clear to both of us that my increasing pain and fever were not going to go away. Each physical examination left me in worse shape—all that pressing and poking wasn't helping my pain or my mind very much. But somehow as the minutes slipped into hours, it was also evident that the attending physician wasn't too sure what was going on either. Unfortunately, the throb was once again sharp and precise. My steadily rising fever was beginning to show itself in intermittent verbal confusion and sluggishness. I tearfully rocked myself gently back and forth on my narrow length of stretcher. (By the fourth history and physical, it's only fair to state, my temper was also running a little short!)

The worst part was that I was beginning to hallucinate, as had often occurred with high fevers in my childhood. As the mind trips got worse and my hold on "reality" lightened, I remember asking my friend to pray for me, and began explaining where and how to touch and stroke me. I felt that I needed to ground myself with another human being as I've never needed to before. Now she's both a fine mother and a nurse, and quite familiar with Therapeutic Touch, but she had never "officially" done it before. But that night as she would comfort me and bring me cool washcloths for my head, we talked each other through a rather fine healing session.

By the time a second friend joined us, though I still looked a wreck, I knew the healing process had begun. My energy field was still very weak, my tears were still flowing, and I was still rocking myself and my stretcher, but the transfer of energy, subtle and profound as always, was evident to me. I felt the pain drawn down through my legs and out of my body; I had begun to relax and found myself emotionally calm and spiritually hopeful. In other words, she had really helped!

We brought our mutual friend up to date on my events of the day. Then I had my second nurse-healing of the day. It was the classic process by an experienced Therapeutic Touch practitioner (see Krieger, 1979).

There was a decided difference between their techniques and the results—the second friend had, after all, trained for many years in Therapeutic Touch. She had a sense of self-confidence and self-understanding that made the experience more refined. She directed her energies very steadily and consistently. Her years of experience were evident to me in the dynamics of the energy flow. She could more clearly direct her energies to various parts, levels, and patterns of my energy field (Rogers, 1970; Nagelberg-Gerhard, 1974). I could feel the surges of energy as we worked together as a trio. And I *mean* it; we were working together—as a trio.

The real difference between their levels of activity was that the more advanced healer was the more powerful. With both of them, though, I as the healee was more actively involved in the Therapeutic Touch process than I had previously anticipated or experienced.

Needless to say, I rapidly responded on many levels, and as I remained on two weeks of bedrest, with IVs, systemic antibiotics, and the rest of the medically called-for yang-type regimen, "we" continued on with the Therapeutic Touch, the nurse-healer's yin approach. And I'm most happy to report, they work together very well (Randolph, 1979).

Self-care: Going with the Flow

All of the body is the mind, but not all of the mind is the body.
                    —Swami Rama
                    (Pelletier and Peper, 1977)

Taking responsibility for one's own health through self-care practices is a traditional nursing concept integrated into most nursing frameworks (Orem, 1971; Rohweder, 1975). However, a person viewed as a multidimensional energy field in mutual simultaneous interaction with the environmental field is an exciting new world view (Rogers, 1970).

Therapeutic Touch, the using of one's hands to help and to heal another, fits into Rogers' framework and can be used in tandem with other holistic health practices (Krieger, 1974/1975, 1979). Evidence for this new world view can be seen in many fields. As Capra (1975) has observed, modern physics and ancient belief systems are convergent upon the same paradigm, a view of the universe as an open system in a continuous dynamic energy flow.

Fine, you say, but how does this relate to self-care practices? Well, if there is a natural orderly pattern in the universe and I'm a living being, it makes sense to follow the paths that lead to balance and harmony. For many, this path includes holistic health practices as well as spiritual development. In addition, the study of ancient and modern teachings helps us to understand the "how" and "why" of this paradigm.

As a nurse-healer, I am aware of nursing's rapid expansion of this new world view (Alfano, 1971; Giacquinta, 1975; Hastings, 1974; Kohnke, 1978; Krieger, 1974/1975, 1979; Mancino, 1977; Nagelberg-Gerhard, 1974, 1975a, b; Randolph, 1979; Rogers, 1970).

For myself, the study of the science of unitary man and Therapeutic Touch has led to a more holistic life-style. I find that I am increasingly able to make healthful changes in myself and in my environment. There have been changes that free up bound energy, changes that promote physical health and well-being, and changes that provide outlets for creativity. The particular avenues are not as important, perhaps, as a willingness to look into the dark areas and illuminate them. And, after all, isn't "light" another form of energy?

The hospitalization experience has allowed me to be at the receiving end of the health care system, rather than at the giving end. No matter how many learning labs you practice in, you can't understand how helpless one can feel when stuck between the siderails of a narrow stretcher with no call button in sight; or how nasty and painful one feels after the fifth "accidental" bumping of a bed by the very same "helpful?" nurse!

In summary, this chapter is a personalized retrospective look at the healer–healee interplay. It was analogous to looking into a mirror for the first time. I saw a person I'd never "seen" before.

Haiku: Why Am I Man?

I am man to sing
the chordal harmony
of universal chimes.
—Marsha Jane Nagelberg-Gerhard

Bibliography

Alfano, G. Healing or caretaking—which will it be? *Nursing Clinics of North America*, 1971, 6, 273–280.

Capra, F. *The tao of physics*. Berkeley: Shambhala Publications, 1975.

Giacquinta, B. *Matrices II lecture series*: New York University, Division of Nursing, 1975.

Hastings Oelbaum, C. Hallmarks of adult wellness. *American Journal of Nursing*, 1974, 74, 1623–1625.

Kohnke, M. *The case for consultation in nursing—designs for professional practice*. New York: John Wiley & Sons, 1978.

Krieger, D. *Matrices I & II lecture series*: New York University, Division of Nursing, Fall 1974 and Spring 1975.

Krieger, D. *The Therapeutic Touch: how to use your hands to help and to heal*. Englewood Cliffs, N.J.: Prentice-Hall, 1979.

Krippner, S. and Villoldo, A. *The realms of healing*. Millbrae, California: Celestial Arts, 1976.

Mancino, D. *Nursing science care plan*. Unpublished manuscript, August, 1977 (available from D. Mancino, 655 6th Avenue, rm 215, N.Y., N.Y. 10010.

Nagelberg-Gerhard, M.J. *Why am I man? Am I the same as my neighbor?* Unpublished manuscript, Fall 1974 (available from M.J. Nagelberg-Gerhard, 180 Summit Ave., #4H, Summit, N.J., 07901).

Nagelberg-Gerhard, M.J. *Beginning exploration of innovative forms of nursing intervention* based on the interplay of man/environment energy transactions. *for the maximizing of "health" of people in our rapidly changing universe*. Unpublished manuscript, May 23, 1975a (available from M.J. Nagelberg-Gerhard, 180 Summit Ave., #4H, Summit, N.J., 07901).

Nagelberg-Gerhard, M.J. *A nursing science conceptual model of resonating patterns of behavior based on man/environment interactions*. Unpublished manuscript, Fall 1975B (available from M.J. Nagelberg-Gerhard, 180 Summit Ave., #4H, Summit, N.J., 07901).

Pelletier, K. and Peper, E. The chutzpah factor in altered states of consciousness. *Journal of Humanistic Psychology*, 1977, 17, 63–73.

Orem, D. *Nursing: concepts of practice*. New York: McGraw-Hill Book Company, 1971.

Ram Dass. *The only dance there is*. Garden City, N.Y.: Doubleday, 1974.

Randolph, G. The Yin-Yang of clinical practice. *Topics in Clinical Nursing*, 1979, 1, 31–41.

Rogers, M. *An introduction to the theoretical basis of nursing*. Philadelphia: F.A. Davis, 1970.

Rohweder, N. *Scientific foundations of nursing*, 3rd edition. New York: J.B. Lippincott Company, 1975.

Samuels, M. and Samuels, N. *Seeing with the mind's eye—the history, techniques and uses of visualization*. New York: Random House, 1975.

Toben, B. *Space-time and beyond*. New York: E.P. Dutton and Co., Inc., 1975.

Chapter 19

Assessing the Effects of Therapeutic Touch through Creative Imagery Techniques

Patricia Heidt

Image Disease/Discomfort is a diagnostic tool which uses patients' drawings and discussions as a basis for exploring their attitudes toward being ill. As modeled after Image-Ca (Achterberg and Lawlis, 1978)* a tape recording is used to assist the patient to relax each body part and to take a "mental journey" through the body. Following this, the patient is instructed to draw (1) what they imagined about their disease/discomfort, (2) how their body is getting rid of it, and (3) how their treatment is assisting them to get well again. Then the therapist and patient explore together the above components of the drawing in order to get a more clear and accurate description of the patient's imagery.

In this chapter, Image Disease/Discomfort is used to assess three patients' attitudes toward their illness while receiving intervention by Therapeutic Touch. The patients' drawings and excerpts from the interviews are presented, followed by the investigator's observations and implications for future research in Therapeutic Touch.

The Patients: Drawings and Interviews

Phil Caleb (see Chapter 15) is a retired U.S.A.F. pilot. He received Therapeutic Touch during a ten-day healing workshop, usually two

*The author wishes to thank Jeanne Achterberg for her assistance in developing Image Disease/Discomfort.

times daily for approximately ten minutes. On Day 5 of the workshop, he drew Figure 1, and an excerpt of the interview which followed is presented:

Ns: Describe how your illness looks in your mind's eye.
Pt: I see a screw-up in the DNA partly. Something outside and in me acting in some fashion to militate toward pathology. My eyes are limited. There is scar tissue on the retina. In the right eye between the optic nerve and the retina a cyst developed and ruptured, according to the doctor. I have lost some sense of peripheral vision. In the left eye there are two small scars. Sometimes I see a kaleidoscope of colors.... It looks like a gray mass that is thick in the middle and thin along the edges, a medium-gray mass. It is not malevolent, I mean not a horribly hideous thing that has happened. Scars on other parts of the body disappear, why can't they here? The scar tissue is like a bad patch job; it is raised, and it is occluding light.... It is getting thinner as new tissue is being regenerated and replaces the scar tissue.
Ns: How do you see your body helping it go away?
Pt: I visualize the scar tissue getting smaller and the retina regenerating. Everything I have learned says this is not possible. I sometimes visualize that around the edges it is breaking up, and going into the bloodstream and being assimilated.... I am lazy when it comes to my eye muscles. I have been in such a habit of not using them and turning my head that I forget sometimes.... I haven't been working on the left eye enough. I realize if I take the time to relax and visualize it will help, but sometimes days go by and I forget.
Ns: How does your treatment work to get rid of the disease?
Pt: It goes against all tradition. I mean consciously I really thought there was no hope for me. (long pause) Treatment is not a good word for me. I am being "worked upon" by a group of people who really like me. They think I have the capability to receive what is happening to me and going off with it. It's not a treatment. It is more than that. You could say it is a growth experience, toward wholeness.

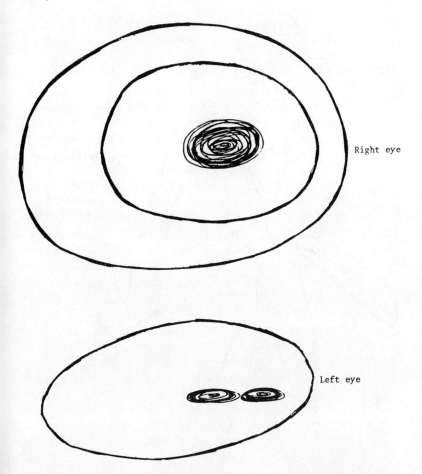

Figure 1. Drawn by Phil on Day 5 of the
Therapeutic Touch workshop.

Several weeks after the healing workshop, Phil drew Figure 2.
An excerpt of the dialogue is as follows:

Ns: Describe how your illness now looks in your mind's eye.

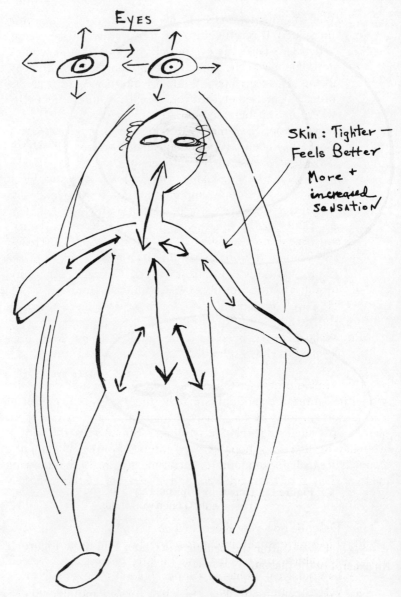

Figure 2. Drawn by Phil several weeks after
the Therapeutic Touch workshop.

Pt: Well, my mental images of my disease have become more integrated. It is difficult to put into words how this occurs. When I visualize my eye muscles and "work" on them, I am somehow at the same time conscious of the pathology in the rest of my body. While my internal energy may be primarily focused on the eyes, there is a spinoff effect elsewhere, like an increased sensation of energy.

Ns: How do you see your body working to make it go away?

Pt: There has been a tremendous change in my self-image. I consistently sense myself throughout the day. Intuitively I can consider healing taking place at several different levels: physically, psychically, and emotionally. . . . I haven't done my "image work" yet—the blind spots in my eyes I am leaving alone for the time being. The reason for this is that I must finish processing what happened at Pumpkin Hollow and become thoroughly comfortable and confident of the changes within me. I think it will take several weeks for me to adjust to the intensity of the experience there.

Ns: How well do you see your treatment working to get rid of the disease?

Pt: Well, there has been no exacerbation, and my confidence level is growing fast indeed.

Chris Lukasiewicz (see Chapter 16) is a woman whose illness disrupted her entire life for approximately three years. A diagnosis of lead poisoning done by hair analysis finally indicated a treatment plan that provided some relief of symptoms. She was a participant in a ten-day healing workshop, received intervention by Therapeutic Touch twice daily for ten minutes each time. Figure 3 is her drawing made on Day 2 of the workshop, and an excerpt of the interview which followed is presented:

Ns: Describe how your illness looks in your mind's eye.

Pt: Pipes have something to do with what illness means to me. My illness interrupted my thinking process and created psychological problems. People couldn't believe how sick I was; they thought I was just tense. I became afraid and like a social recluse. As a student I also withdrew: blockage! The pipes are like my body, which is full of poisonous

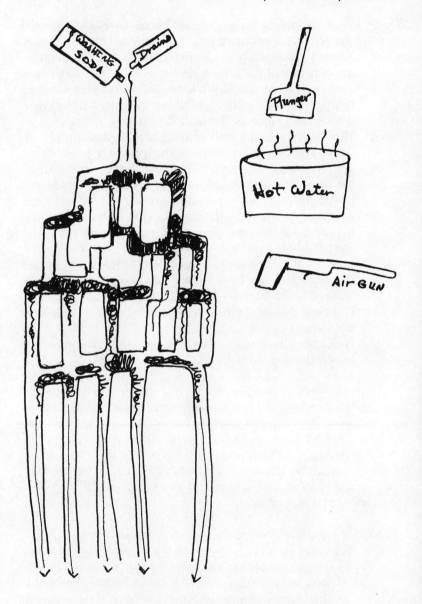

Figure 3. Drawn by Chris on Day 2 of the
Therapeutic Touch workshop.

toxins, and this kept me from functioning normally. My GI tract was blocked, and this led to a buildup of lead and copper. My enzyme system was blocked and food could not be digested, so I lost weight. Lead began to accumulate in the soft tissues and bone structure organs. There is a lot of blockage. It is like gunk, garbage, unpleasant stuff.... There is a lot of blockage left, as you can see here in my picture. It can be dissolved. I can get rid of it. It comes out the kidneys and intestines.

Ns: How do you see your body helping it go away?

Pt: There is a chemical process going on by taking calcium verconate. The zinc and nutrients I ingest dissolve the gunk, and it acts like a plunger in that it sucks in and pulls it out. After the first intravenous treatment, my mind cleared up.... I see Therapeutic Touch as an energy coming in and washing out the gunk too. As I feel more relaxed I am breathing deeper. I inhale "blue energy" and it seems as though my self-confidence increases. I have felt angry and allowed myself to be intimidated for some time. It is good to feel more forgiving now.

Ns: How well do you see your treatment working to get rid of the disease?

Pt: Therapeutic Touch is very potent. It is working in a very powerful way in me. I know that it takes a long time for the chemical process to clean things out and I would like to speed this process up. I decided to use some more instruments like the air gun (pointing to picture). It's like an energy treatment to fight the doubts within myself.

On Day 9 of treatment by Therapeutic Touch, Chris drew Figure 4. An excerpt of the interview which followed is presented:

Ns: Describe how your illness now looks in your mind's eye.

Pt: The blockage is clearing up. The gunk is moving slowly but consistently. Some of the pipes are even clear, as you can see here. The blockage in my life is clearing.... These pipes are representing the physical, social, and psychological parts of myself. Three months ago I felt so bad I was prepared to die. Now, I want to see my friends and go back

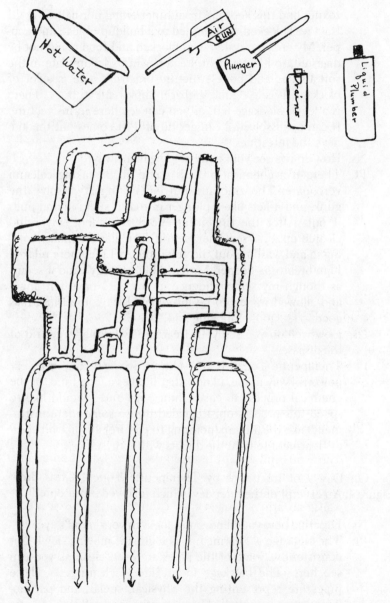

Figure 4. Drawn by Chris on Day 9 of the
Therapeutic Touch workshop.

to school. I have energy to fix my apartment. It seems the major change is that the disabling restrictions are gone pretty much.

Ns: How do you see your body helping it go away?

Pt: It is slow, like healing. I have been walking a lot and my strength has increased tremendously. I have felt like doing some healing with others myself. I see my body slowly healing itself. I do deep breathing during Therapeutic Touch and it is like the energy moves through my head—blue clear water moving through my head, down through my body, through the solar plexus, and out.

Ns: How is the treatment you are receiving working to get rid of the disease?

Pt: When I receive energy through healing, it increases the removal of the toxins. I feel much less fatigue. My body processes are being stimulated to move the gunk out through the normal means. I'm just way ahead now.

E.T. is a 28-year-old hospitalized patient with a "problem of the kneecap," as he describes it. His diagnosis is sarcoma and when the interview took place, he had become very demanding and regressed in his needs, according to hospital staff. He had been in the hospital six weeks when Figure 5 was drawn. An excerpt of the interview that followed is presented:

Ns: Describe how your disease looks in your mind's eye.

Pt: There are clumps of disease trying to destroy my kneecap: little beads of disease, like in a petri dish, in the joints which cause pus and destroy tissue in the knee. I don't know what is going on. Every day there is something different, and the doctors disagree now on the treatment. I'm insecure because my arm is swollen and my temperature has now gone way up (E.T. begins to cry and it is several minutes before the interview continues). . . . I don't know how strong it is. I can feel just great and then the doctors turn around and say they have to operate.

Ns: How do you see your body helping it go away?

Pt: I am taking antibiotics. I don't know what they do. . . . (E.T. beings to cry again, and I terminate the interview. I

Figure 5.   Drawn by E.T. after six weeks in
the hospital.

spend ten minutes using Therapeutic Touch intervention
with him, and massage both his feet.)

On the next three consecutive days, Therapeutic Touch was
administered for approximately ten minutes once each day. On the
third day, E.T. drew Figure 6, and an excerpt of the interview that
followed is presented:

Figure 6.   Drawn by E.T. after three days of
Therapeutic Touch intervention.

Ns:. How do you see your illness now in your mind's eye?

Pt: Well, my leg feels a little better today. Some of the pain is
gone. It looks like they are going to operate soon. . . . This
picture is me running. I'm exercising at home. My wife and
I are running along the boardwalk, trying to get some exercise. I'm a track man and going just as fast as I can.

Ns: How do you see your body helping you to get better?

Pt: I'm not sure yet. I'm depressed because I want to be home
with my wife. You know this whole thing started just after
I got married, a year ago. It seems like I've been sick most
of my marriage. My mother was really upset about the
whole thing, my getting married, I mean. She and my wife
just do not get along. . . . She kept calling, and it was interfering. . . . She's been a wonderful person to me all my life,
you know. She got me through college and everything. But
it got too much, playing referee between those two. I finally

had to face her. I just had to put my foot down. . . . It was very hard for me.

Ns: How do you see your treatment working to get rid of the disease?

Pt: I'm confused about the treatment. There are lots of doctors on my case, and they seem to disagree on exactly what should go on right now. It is hard for me to feel hopeful about anything happening. I am tired much of the time. (E.T. spends some time talking about fears of losing his new job because of time missed and his loneliness in the hospital.)

Discussion

In this chapter there is no attempt to obtain an imagery score as is done with Image-Ca (Achterberg and Lawlis, 1978). Observations of patients' drawings and excerpted interview data do indicate that changes took place between the first and second interviews. All three patients receiving Therapeutic Touch responded to this intervention in their own unique way, and generalizations cannot be made from this small sample. However, some commonalities emerged and may prove of interest for future research in the area of Therapeutic Touch.

Wholeness

In Phil's drawings and interviews, there is a change from focus on the site of pathology (eyes) to the whole body's involvement in the healing process. He says, "Therapeutic Touch is a growth experience toward wholeness. . . . Healing is taking place at different levels. Chris says that the pipes in her drawings represent her total body, that is "physical, social, and psychological parts of myself." She continues, "The blockage in my life is clearing." E.T.'s drawings also shift from site of pathology (leg) to his whole body in movement.

In holistic health care, illness is viewed, not primarily as a physical problem, but as a response of the whole person. Wellness demands that the whole person be mobilized to participate in treatment for lasting effects. It is significant that these patients talked about and drew healing processes taking place in the whole body. How does intervention by Therapeutic Touch help patients to become aware that illness is more than a "physical problem"? Is one of the effects of Therapeutic Touch an increase in compassion toward self and others, which facilitates a belief system about illness/wellness based on "whole-istic" ideas of care? Future research in Therapeutic Touch could study those factors in the healer–healee interaction which enhance healing the whole person.

Belief Systems

During the second interviews with Phil and Chris, the feelings of "no hope" were giving way to a more joyful expectancy of wellness. Chris says there is a change from a feeling of being closed in or "intimidation" to an openness and self-confidence that allows her to participate in her own healing process more quickly. Similarly, Phil states, "there has been a tremendous change in my self-image. . . . Therapeutic Touch goes against all tradition. I really thought there was no hope for me."

E.T. is less depressed on the second interview and is able to express the anger and fears involved in being sick and hospitalized. He had received an explanation about Therapeutic Touch, but remained rather skeptical. He does not see any relationship between the drawing of his "sick leg" and his statement that "I finally just had to put my foot down." More treatment is necessary to assist him to "work through" the emotions that may have predisposed him to becoming ill. It is noted that skepticism does not necessarily interfere with the effects of Therapeutic Touch, as long as there is some openness to the healing interaction.

Izard and Tomkins (1966) state that it is the emotions that provide the blueprint for rational thought and action and are part of the "image" each of us carries within ourselves motivating us toward goal-seeking behavior. As patients learn how feelings affect levels of wellness, sickness may be changed from a "bad thing" to more of an opportunity for self-growth and renewal.

Further exploration into the relationship between belief systems and intervention by Therapeutic Touch could be helpful. What part does patient expectation play in changing attitudes toward illness? What factors within the healer–healee relationship facilitate change in belief systems? How does "care and concern" on the part of the healer affect the healing process? What is the relationship between healer's self-esteem and the effects of Therapeutic Touch? What is the relationship between the healer's belief system and the effects of Therapeutic Touch?

Relaxation

E.T. says there is less pain in his leg and he draws himself as running. Chris says she is less fatigued, is walking more, and wants to get involved in usual daily activities. Phil talks about a "spinoff effect" of Therapeutic Touch on the energy level of his entire body.

Research in Therapeutic Touch indicates the potential of this intervention for eliciting in the patient a state of physiological relaxation (Krieger, Peper, and Ancoli, 1979) and decreasing level of anxiety (Heidt, 1979). Relaxation helps the body's constricted functioning to regain its normal self-regulatory activities. Relaxation is a way of unstressing, breaking the cycle of tension and fear, and allowing the person to enlarge his/her perspectives. Further research could assess the effects of this intervention on levels of pain and anxiety in a variety of clinical environments.

Image Disease/Discomfort

The preceding dialogues indicate that using creative imagery to measure patients' attitudes toward their illness differs from the traditional therapist–patient interview model. The patient is asked to suspend rational stereotypical responses toward expressing their attitudes in favor of "picturing" and "drawing" first. Reporting comes later. The attempt here is to assist the patient to recognize the emotional context of the illness and to give as much credence to this aspect as to the more intellectual, logical thought sequences of the interview data.

No attempt was made to go beyond the assessment level with the data, although the patients' drawings and interviews provide possibilities for treatment. Future research could use this tool to assess the effects of Therapeutic Touch on patients' progress at regular intervals over longer periods of time. Present health care systems utilizing imagery for assessment and treatment compare drawings from initial sessions with drawings of follow-up sessions to see how patients' belief systems and attitudes toward illness change (Simonton, Simonton, and Creighton, 1978).

No work has been done with imagery to assess the therapist–healer's attitudes toward what is taking place during the intervention process. Future research could assess changes in the healer's imagery over a period of time, to obtain information about the process of teaching and learning to administer Therapeutic Touch.

Summary

This chapter presents one approach to assessing the attitudes of patients toward their illness as they receive intervention by Therapeutic Touch. Some suggestions for further research are given.

Bibliography

Achterberg, J. and Lawlis, G.F. *Imagery of cancer.* Champaign, Ill.: Institute for Personality and Ability Testing, 1978.

Green, E. and Green, A. *Beyond biofeedback.* New York: Dell, 1977.

Heidt, P. The effects of Therapeutic Touch on anxiety level of hospitalized patients. Unpublished Doctoral Dissertation, New York University, 1979.

Izard, C. E. and Tomkins, S. S. Affect and behavior: anxiety as a negative effect. *In* C. D. Spielberger (Ed.), *Anxiety and behavior.* New York: Academic Press, 1966, pp. 81–125.

Klinger, E. *Structure and function of fantasy.* New York: Wiley-Interscience, 1971.

Krieger, D. Healing by the laying-on of hands as a facilitator of bioenergetic change: the response of in-vivo human hemoglobin. *Psychoenergetics,* 1974, *1*, 121–129.

Krieger, D. Therapeutic Touch: the imprimatur of nursing. *American Journal of Nursing,* 1975, *5*, 784–787.

Krieger, D., Peper, E. and Ancoli, S. Therapeutic Touch: searching for evidence of physiological change. *American Journal of Nursing,* 1979, 79, (4), 660–662.

Marks, D.F. Individual differences in the vividness of visual imagery and their effect on function. *In* P.W. Sheehan (Ed.), *Function and nature of imagery.* New York: Academic Press, 1972, pp. 234–249.

Simonton, C. O., Simonton, S. M., and Creighton, J. *Getting well again.* Los Angeles: J.P. Tarcher, 1978.

Conclusion

Patricia Heidt

While preparing the chapter that summarized Krieger's research, my fingers hit the typewriter keys, writing out "...there was a rise in hemogloving level...." Of course, I had meant to type "hemoglobin level." I paused, looked at this interesting typing error, and recalled comments of workshop participants when I was teaching about Therapeutic Touch. One time a woman asked me, "Aren't you talking about TLC [tender loving care]?" Another participant queried, "Aren't you really saying this is love?" and another stated, "This is nothing new; nurses have always been taught to have empathy toward their patients." When I was becoming acquainted with the conceptual framework upon which Therapeutic Touch is built, I had the same kinds of questions. I had always known that my patients felt better after I cared for them, but I wondered how this caring could produce changes in their physiological and/or psychological responses.

One of the most intriguing aspects of Therapeutic Touch was that it was a way for me to bridge the gap between psychology and physics. This framework also provided information on a scientific level about a subject that I had traditionally believed was religious or mystical. I sensed that this union of knowledge was a necessary part of my evolution as a person and a health practitioner. With the assumption that man is an open system of streaming energies, the outer layer of my skin could no longer be considered the boundary or end of my personal space. As I more fully realized that all living organisms are continuously interacting with each other, exchanging matter, energy, and information, I also knew that we are not nearly so separate as Western physical and psychological concepts would have us believe. And it is the desire to help another (or the love on the part of the helper) that mobilizes these energies for healing interactions to take place.

Kunz (1978) has stated that in all traditions the healing person has always recognized that there is an order and a harmony in the universe that is bigger than oneself. The role of the healer is to synchronize his/her own personal field with that larger universal energy force and to act as a channel or conduit for the flow of these energies to the person in need. It is in moments of quiet centeredness that this is most easily accomplished. Our contributors describe the evolution within themselves that allowed the development of this healing environment to take place. In the manuscripts which form this book of readings, it is evident that the authors practice Therapeutic Touch out of a sense of care and concern for themselves and for others. Healing for them is not considered a "paranormal phenomenon," but rather a recognition of the innate human potentials that characterize all persons. In the description of their healing experiences, both practitioners and receivers of Therapeutic Touch share a joyfulness in the discovery or rediscovery of the tremendous capacities within themselves for growth and healing.

This kind of awareness, coupled with a motivation to participate in one's own healing processes, is often termed "transformation." When many individuals begin to live and work in this transformed way, there are tremendous possibilities for change in our society. Borrowing a phrase from Weber's chapter (p. 36), we can live as if in a "moving meditation." We invite our readers to continue this book in their own personal way.

Bibliography

Kunz, D. Healing Workshop. Craryville, New York, 1978.

Index